Michael O'C

Love

Mom & Dad

93.12.25.

THE LIFE AND TIMES OF
CHARLES DICKENS

THE LIFE AND TIMES OF
CHARLES DICKENS

ALAN S. WATTS

CRESCENT BOOKS
New York

PHOTOGRAPHIC ACKNOWLEDGEMENTS

The publishers would like to thank the following for permission to reproduce the photographs and illustrations in this book:

Dickens House Museum, London: 3, 11, 14, 16, 17, 18, 19 (top), 20, 21 (left and right), 22, 23, 24 (bottom left), 25, 27, 28, 30, 31 (top), 40 (top), 42 (left), 46 (right), 47 (top), 49 (top left and right), 50, 51 (top), 54, 55, 65 (bottom), 69 (right), 70, 71, 77 (top), 78 (bottom), 79, 83, 85, 86, 87, 89 (bottom), 90, 92, 95, 97, 98, 102, 105 (top), 106, 117, 119, 125, 127, 128, 129, 133, 134 (top left), 136, 139, 140, 141, 142, 143. The Bridgeman Art Library, London: 60 (bottom); 63 (top), Chateau Blerancourt/ Giraudon; 68 (top), Bradford Art Galleries & Museums; 91 (top), Bradford City Art Gallery & Museums; 96, Musee des Beaux Arts, Valenciennes/Giraudon; 103 (bottom), Forbes Magazine Collection; 110, Galerie Dijol, Paris/Giraudon; 116 (top), Musee Carnavelet, Paris/Lauros-Giraudon; 132 (top), Royal Holloway & Bedford New College, Surrey. The Mary Evans Picture Library, London: 101 (top). David Drummond's theatre bookshop, *Pleasure of Past Times*, London: 19 (bottom), 21 (centre), 24 (bottom right), 31 (bottom), 43 (bottom), 51 (bottom), 80 (bottom), 105 (bottom), 115 (top left), 126 (bottom), 134 (top right), 138 (left), 142, 143. National Maritime Museum, Greenwich: 12 (bottom), 15 (top right), 35 (bottom), 60 (top). National Portrait Gallery/Tate Gallery, London: 10. The Perkins Institution for the Blind, Boston, USA: 62. Chris Davies, Photographer, London: 45 (bottom), 47 (bottom). Royal Doulton Limited: 142 (top right), 143 (top centre). Stills from the films *Oliver Twist*, *A Tale of Two Cities* and *Great Expectations* by courtesy of the Rank Organisation Plc, and BFI Stills, Posters and Designs, London: 40 (bottom), 41 (bottom), 43 (top), 113 (bottom), 115 (top right), 120 (bottom), 121 (bottom); BFI Stills, Posters and Designs, London: BFI/Vitagraph Corporation: 36·(bottom); BFI/Renown: 37 (bottom); BFI/Heindale Weintraub: 45 (right), 46 (left), 49 (bottom), 51 (bottom right); BFI/MGM: 77 (bottom), 78 (top), 93 (centre); BFI/20th Century Fox: 82, 89 (top), 93 (top and bottom); BFI/Transcontinental: 121 (centre), 122 (top), 123; BFI/Universal: 132 (bottom); Sands Films, London: 107.

This edition published 1991 by Crescent Books
Distributed by Outlet Book Company, Inc.
A Random House Company
225, Park Avenue South
New York, New York 10003.

First published 1991 by Studio Editions Ltd.
Princess House, 50 Eastcastle Street,
London W1N 7AP, England.

Designed by Watermark Communications Group Ltd.,
Chesham, England.

ISBN 0-517-05917-7

Printed and bound in Czechoslovakia.

8 7 6 5 4 3 2 1

CONTENTS

Charles Dickens, 1852

FOREWORD

I have attempted to do a number of things in this book. First, I have tried to give a brief account of Dickens's life, together with an idea of his character and his interests other than writing. Secondly, I have sought to describe some of the developments taking place during his lifetime and the social problems he confronted. Thirdly, I have hoped to arouse an interest in his novels amongst readers who may have little or no knowledge of them, or to re-kindle an interest where it may have lapsed. And lastly, I have wished to demonstrate by reference to the many plays and films based on the novels, and the variety of 'collectables' – such as cigarette cards and figurines – illustrating Dickens characters, what a pervasive and continuing influence Dickens has had upon our culture.

I hope that my text, which has been written with the general reader in mind, will encourage many to wish to know more and seek out more detailed and scholarly books on Dickens. I hope, too, that the illustrations will supplement the text and that the captions to the illustrations will add a further layer of information and interest. Having observed that books on Dickens tend to contain the same pictures (which to some extent is inevitable), wherever I have had a choice, I have selected unfamiliar ones.

I have realised, too, that many readers, especially younger ones, would be greatly helped in reading a Dickens novel for the first time if they knew something of the plot in advance. I have therefore compiled a short synopsis of each of the fifteen major novels. This has not been easy because the novels are long, their plots are involved with many sub-plots; I have ignored most of the sub-plots and concentrated instead on the main narratives.

If I may make a suggestion to newcomers to Dickens, it is best to begin (in my opinion) with one of the shorter and less-complex books. Try *Oliver Twist* or *Great Expectations*.

Finally, let me explain my stance. I feel that so much attention has been given of late to Dickens's private life that the general public might be in danger of forgetting that his importance to posterity is as a novelist. In Dickens's case, being a novelist meant much more than writing stories for entertainment. He looked upon himself as a fighter against injustice and stupidity, against snobbery, against false ideas in education and government, and indeed against cruelty and unkindness in all forms. He wrote *The Chimes* to 'strike a great blow for the poor', and *Bleak House* to denounce the Court of Chancery.

I have therefore concentrated on this public side of Dickens, and have made only brief references to his separation from his wife and his affair with Ellen Ternan. Of course, these events need to be taken into account when assessing Dickens's character, but enough has been written about them recently. In these pages I wish to describe Dickens the novelist, the reformer, the actor, the public reader, the man of incredible energy and inventiveness – in his own words, 'The Inimitable Boz'.

A.S.W.

A RESTLESS LIFE

CHAPTER
1

A RESTLESS LIFE

A man's life can often be summarised by stating where he was born and where he died. The fact that Dickens was born in a small terrace-house in Portsmouth and died in a fair-sized country villa on Gad's Hill, near Rochester, indicates that he was certainly a financial success. When one looks at the variety of houses that he occupied between these two, contrasts the squalid lodging in Lant Street with the magnificent Palazzo Peschiere in Genoa, and remembers the secret chalet in Condette, near Boulogne, one begins to have an inkling of the range of his experiences and the fascination of his character.

This chapter is intended to present a

JOHN DICKENS (1785–1851) *(above), father of Charles Dickens. A jovial and improvident man, he was portrayed by Dickens as Mr Micawber and, more sombrely, as William Dorrit. He was imprisoned for debt in 1824, and died after enduring an agonising operation.*

THE NICKLEBY PORTRAIT *(far left) by Daniel Maclise, an engraving of which was used as the frontispiece for* Nicholas Nickleby. *G.A. Sala called it "the excellent delineation of the young man with long silky hair . . . the fascinating smile, the marvellously clear and enquiring eyes . . ."*

ELIZABETH DICKENS (1789–1863) *(top left), mother of Charles. Her father, Charles Barrow, was Chief Conductor of Monies in Town at the Navy Pay Office. For some years he systematically embezzled the funds and, on being discovered, fled abroad.*

SOMERSET HOUSE *(left). In 1805 Dickens's father, John Dickens, was appointed clerk in the Navy Pay Office.*

brief life of Dickens. Because subsequent chapters contain many biographical details relating to his works and the circumstances in which they were written, it is interesting to draw the outline of his biography by recounting the many places which at one time or another he called home.

Charles Dickens was born on Friday, 7 February 1812, at No.1, Mile End Terrace, Landport, Portsmouth. The house is now maintained by the local authority and is open to the public. In 1812 it was described in a newspaper advertisement as "a modern well-built dwelling-house" comprising "in the basement, a good kitchen and cellar; ground floor, two excellent parlours; first floor, two good bedrooms, and two garrets in the attic . . . The Premises are 18 feet in width, and 120 feet in depth."

Charles's father, John Dickens, a clerk in the Navy Pay Office, had previously been employed at Somerset House, London. But in November 1807 he had been transferred to Portsmouth. In 1810, a daughter, Fanny, was born. Then came Charles in 1812. A few months later, the family moved first to Hawke Street and then to Wish Street. In 1815 John Dickens was transferred back to London, and Charles entered his first London home. Although there is no positive proof of where this was, it is believed to have been at 10 Norfolk Street, a house to which he would eventually return some years later. It still stands but is now 22 Cleveland Street.

On New Year's Day 1817 the family

ORDNANCE TERRACE, *Chatham, where Charles Dickens lived from 1817 to 1822. On 3 March 1820 a disastrous fire broke out in a bakehouse in the High Street. It spread rapidly and some fifty-three houses and thirteen warehouses were destroyed. John Dickens wrote an account of it which was published in* The Times. *He served on a relief committee following the fire, and donated two guineas to help those who had suffered.*

moved again, and after a brief sojourn at Sheerness settled at Chatham. There they lived at 2 Ordnance Terrace, another house which may still be seen. Dickens had only the haziest memories of any of his earlier homes, but he retained vivid recollections of this one. There are many scattered references to it in *The Uncommercial Traveller.* In one essay he recalled the playing-field which stretched out in front of the terrace,

MISS TOX WELCOMES THE PARTY (*Dombey and Son*). *2 Ordnance Terrace was a crowded but lively little house with a stimulating atmosphere. There were parties and magic lantern shows.*

where Chatham railway station now stands. He expressed his regret at the way things had changed as a result:

The two beautiful hawthorn-trees, the hedge, the turf, and all those buttercups and daisies, had given place to the stoniest of jolting roads.

In another essay he explained that he had "a very sympathetic nurse, with a large circle of married acquaintances" and "was taken to so many lyings-in that I wonder I escaped becoming a professional martyr to

16 BAYHAM STREET (*left*), *Camden Town, London, where the Dickens family came to live when they left Chatham in 1822. Charles followed later, arriving "packed, like game" in the coach, Timpson's Blue-Eyed Maid, late in December. He was very hurt at finding that there were no plans for him to resume his education. "What would I have given . . . to have been sent back to any other school, to have been taught anything, anywhere!"*

them in after-life". This nurse, Mary Weller, was the young lady responsible for relating the bloodcurdling tales of Captain Murderer and Chips the Carpenter which, though giving him "nightmares and perspirations", were to be important items in his imaginative stock-in-trade.

It was a crowded little house, accommodating John and Elizabeth Dickens, Mrs Dickens's widowed sister, Mary Allen, the two maids, Mary Weller and Jane Bonny, and five children. But it was a happy, stimulating home. There were parties where the children would be hoisted on the table to sing. There were magic lantern shows. Here little Charles fell in love with Lucy Stroughill from next door – "a peach-faced creature in a blue sash". Here, too, Charles wrote the very first piece of prose of which a record remains; but only the title, *Misnar,*

Sultan of India – a Tragedy, is known.

John Dickens's financial difficulties began to accumulate in this house. He was a convivial man and loved to entertain his friends. Unfortunately, the Navy's method of payment encouraged him to borrow. He was paid three-monthly and, by the time the next quarter-day arrived, he was having to live on credit.

As an economy measure, the family moved to a smaller house at 18 St Mary's Place, The Brook, a whitewashed house next to the Providence Baptist Chapel. The minister's son, William Giles, kept a school not far away, and here young Charles re-

"THE NAVY AIN'T WHAT IT WAS!", *a coloured lithograph by Engelman Graf, published by Coindet and Co. in 1828. Many soldiers and sailors lost limbs during the French Wars, and men with wooden legs must have been a familiar sight. Dickens has scores of references to wooden legs, the earliest being a tiny note to a school-friend.*

MRS PIPCHIN (*left*) *in* Dombey and Son *was modelled on Mrs Roylance with whom Dickens lodged in Little College Street, during his father's prison sentence.*

WELLINGTON HOUSE ACADEMY (*bottom left*). *After leaving the Blacking Warehouse, Dickens attended Mr Jones's establishment in Mornington Place as a day-scholar. A schoolfellow recalled: "At that time Dickens took to writing small tales . . . he was also very strong in using a sort of lingo which made us quite unintelligible to bystanders. We were very strong, too, in theatricals."*

BOYS AT WELLINGTON HOUSE ACADEMY SOLICITING ALMS, *a drawing by Fred Barnard (bottom right). Dickens's schoolfellow recalled: "I quite remember Dickens on one occasion heading us in Drummond Street in pretending to be poor boys and asking the passers-by for charity – especially old ladies; one of whom told us she 'had no money for beggar boys'."*

CHARLES DICKENS *aged eighteen. This miniature on ivory was painted by Dickens's aunt by marriage, Mrs Janet Barrow, who was probably the original for the character of Miss La Creevy in* Nicholas Nickleby. *It shows Dickens as he appeared while working as a shorthand reporter, at just about the time he met Maria Beadnell.*

ceived his first formal education. But he was not permitted to enjoy the benefit of this for very long, for in 1822, his father – now quite heavily in debt – was sent back to London.

Dickens's next home was 16 Bayham Street, Camden Town, an even smaller house. Although Aunt Mary had left the family, there were now six children, plus an orphan girl from Chatham workhouse and a relative named James Lamert. Charles had remained in Chatham for a little while and was dismayed when he rejoined them. "There was debt in the house," he recorded later. He was not sent to school again. Instead he became a little drudge, running errands, visiting pawnbrokers and, after another move to a large house at 4 Gower

TEMPLE BAR. *"That laden-headed old obstruction."* *"Telison's Bank by Temple Bar was an old-fashioned place, very small, very dark, very ugly, very incommodious."*

Street North, delivering handbills to announce "Mrs Dickens's Academy for Young Ladies". This venture never even started; no enquiries were ever received and the only result was a larger debt. Inevitably, John Dickens was arrested for debt and sent to the Marshalsea Prison. The house was given up, and Mrs Dickens and the younger children moved into the prison with him. Charles, however, having begun a job in a blacking warehouse owned by their relative, James Lamert, could not go with them. So lodgings were found for him with a Mrs Roylance in Little College Street. (Mrs Roylance would later be portrayed as Mrs Pipchin in *Dombey and Son*.) His sister, Fanny, also remained outside the prison; she was currently resident at the Royal Academy of Music. After a while Charles moved to lodgings nearer the prison, at 1 Lant Street, Southwark. When he came to write *The Pickwick Papers* he recalled these lodgings, making them accommodate Bob Sawyer and become the scene of his disastrous party. It was then that he described the population of the street as "migratory, usually disappearing on the verge of quarter-day, and generally by night. His

Majesty's revenues are seldom collected in this happy valley."

John Dickens was released from prison while his son was still working at the blacking warehouse. The whole family now went to Mrs Roylance's. While they were there, John Dickens and James Lamert quarrelled

ENGAGEMENT RING, *gold set with turquoises, given by Dickens to Catherine Hogarth in May 1835.*

MARIA BEADNELL AS A MILKMAID, BY HENRY AUSTIN. *Henry Austin, who later married Dickens's sister, Letitia, painted two pictures of Maria Beadnell. One showed her with her brother, George, as Dido and Ascanius. The other, shown above, depicts her as a milkmaid. Austin gave this picture to Dickens as a present.*

MR PICKWICK ADDRESSES THE CLUB. *"The eloquent Pickwick, with one hand gracefully concealed behind his coat tails, and the other waving in air to assist his glowing declamation: his elevated position revealing those tights and gaiters, which . . . inspired involuntary awe and respect."*

FURNIVAL'S INN. *"When I opened my door in Furnival's Inn to the managing partner who represented the firm [of Chapman and Hall], I recognised in him the person from whom I had bought . . . my first copy of the Magazine in which my first effusion . . . had appeared. I told my visitor of the coincidence which we both hailed as a good omen: and so fell to business."* As a result Dickens *"thought of Mr Pickwick"*.

over the way Charles was being exposed to the public gaze as he worked. So Charles came home and was sent to school. The next year the family moved to 29 Johnson Street and remained there until March 1827, when they were evicted for non-payment of rent. Their next home was at 17 The Polygon, Somers Town.

About this time, Charles left school and went to work at the office of a solicitor, Mr Molloy. After a short spell there he joined the firm of Ellis and Blackmore of Gray's Inn. The family was now frequently on the move. From the Polygon they went to their former house at 10 Norfolk Street, Fitzroy Square; then in 1832 to 15 Fitzroy Street; and in January 1833 to 18 Bentinck Street. Their rooms here were above an upholsterer's shop and were apparently quite spacious. While they were here, Dickens pursued his courtship of Maria Beadnell, on whom he based Dora Spenlow in *David Copperfield*. He also produced an operetta, *Clari*, with friends and members of the family taking the parts. Notices and programmes were specially printed – an indication of the extravagance of the Dickens family which was to lead, in November 1834, to John Dickens being arrested for debt once again and briefly lodged in a sponging-house until his release could be arranged. The Bentinck Street house had to be given up, following which Charles went to lodge at North End, Holborn, before finding chambers at 13 Furnival's Inn, Holborn, on the site of which the Prudential Assurance Company's head office now stands. He had already had bachelor lodgings in Cecil Street and Buckingham Street, as reflected in *David Copperfield*.

His affair with Maria had ended at about the time of the *Clari* production. Soon afterwards, in December 1833, his first short story *A Dinner at Poplar Walk* (later entitled *Mr Minns and his Cousin*) was published in *The Monthly Magazine*. Although it appeared anonymously and Charles received nothing for it, he was so overcome with joy and pride at seeing his work "in all the glory of print" that his eyes "could not bear the street, and were not fit to be seen there". More short stories and sketches were published by other magazines. Some were signed "Boz", the nickname of his small brother, Augustus. Before long, the signature "Boz" was becoming familiar in journalistic circles, and people were enquiring who this new comic writer might be.

Dickens was now working as a reporter on *The Morning Chronicle*. In May 1835 he became engaged to Catherine Hogarth, the daughter of one of his colleagues. The Hogarths lived in Chelsea, an inconvenient

distance from Furnival's Inn, so Dickens took lodgings for the summer at 11 Selwood Terrace, Brompton, so as to be near his fiancée.

The next year saw the transformation of his fortunes with the publication of *The Pickwick Papers*. He could now afford to get married, and on 2 April 1836 the wedding took place at St Luke's, Chelsea. The married couple moved into a larger set of chambers at Furnival's Inn, where they were joined by Catherine's sister, Mary, and Dickens's brother, Fred (not such an unusual arrangement in those days).

Continued success enabled Dickens to give up the Furnival's Inn chambers in March 1837 and lease an entire house at 48 Doughty Street, where he moved after a brief spell in lodgings at 30 Upper Norton Street. Doughty Street was his first "principal" home. Here he began to entertain other leading writers, journalists and artists.

DICKENS DELIVERS HIS FIRST MANUSCRIPT. "*My first effusion – dropped stealthily one evening at twilight, with fear and trembling, into a dark letter-box, in a dark office, up a dark court in Fleet Street.*"

NANCY. *The murder of Nancy was the most dramatic of Dickens's readings, and a popular subject for stage presentations.*

DICKENS *in October 1837, aged 25, portrayed by Samuel Laurence.*

CATHERINE DICKENS *(far right) (1815–1879) as a young woman. Catherine, the eldest daughter of George Hogarth, a colleague of Dickens on* The Morning Chronicle, *was born in Scotland and came to England only a few years before her marriage to Dickens on 2 April 1836. She always retained her Scottish enunciation.*

THE OLD BULL AND MOUTH INN, *St Martins-le-Grand (now pulled down). The England of* The Pickwick Papers *was the England of gallcried inns, post-chaises, turnpikes and coachmen.*

A son had already been born in Furnival's Inn, and in Doughty Street two daughters were added to the family. In the mews across the street Charles kept his first horse and carriage. He hired a manservant, Topping, who was at once groom and general factotum.

Dickens was to have very few principal places of residence – Doughty Street, Devonshire Terrace, Tavistock House, and Gad's Hill Place – but, as the following pages will make clear, a multitude of short-term occupancies. There appears to have been a restlessness in his blood, perhaps inherited from his father, who was constantly moving house.

Number 48 Doughty Street was a four-storey house in a smart road with lodge-gates at either end, and gatekeepers in mulberry livery. It contained a basement with kitchen, still-room and wash-house; the dining-room and morning-room occupied the ground floor; the drawing-room was at the front of the first floor and the room at the rear was probably used as Dickens's writing-room; there were two bedrooms on the second floor and smaller ones in the attics. The house is now the Dickens Museum and is open to the public. Dickens lived there from 1837 to 1839 while engaged on *The Pickwick Papers, Oliver Twist* and *Nicholas Nickleby*. The family had only just settled in when, on 7 May 1837, Catherine's sister, Mary Hogarth, was taken ill and died within a few hours. Dickens and his wife were deeply shocked. Dicken could not apply himself to his work for some weeks and, in order to recover from their sudden loss, he and his wife retreated to Collins's Farm, Hampstead, "to try a fortnight's rest and quiet".

While at Doughty Street, Dickens took several other short holidays besides making trips to Yorkshire in preparation for the Dotheboys Hall episodes in *Nicholas Nickleby*. He went on a tour to the Midlands and

North Wales with his illustrator; spent a week in Manchester with Ainsworth and Forster, and visited Exeter to find a cottage for his parents. The first of many holidays at Broadstairs was taken in early September 1837. In October and November he and Catherine spent a week at the Ship Hotel, Brighton. In the summer of 1838 they rented a cottage in Twickenham, coming home for August before going to the Isle of Wight for ten days at the beginning of September. The next year they took a cottage at Petersham from May to the end of August, and in September were again at Broadstairs. In fact, Dickens was absent from Doughty Street for a large proportion of his tenancy.

He also made a trip to France in July 1837. This was his first visit abroad, the prelude to many cross-channel voyages to come. He and Catherine were accompanied by H.K. Browne (the illustrator "Phiz"). Writing from the Hotel Rignolle in Calais, Dickens reported to Forster:

We arrived here in great state this morning – I very sick, and Missis very well . . . We have arranged for a post coach to take us to Ghent, Brussels, Antwerp, and a hundred other places that I cannot recollect now . . .

After giving up 48 Doughty Street, Dickens

moved to 1 Devonshire Terrace. This was a detached house in what is now Marylebone Road. In one of his letters, Dickens gave the following particulars about it:

On the ground floor: Square Entrance-hall, Library, Dining-room, Breakfast-room.
First Floor: Drawing-room, best bedroom, second bedroom, Water closet.
Second Floor: Day nursery or large common sitting-room, Night nursery, or bedroom with two beds. Female servants' bedroom.
Attic: Man's room.
Basement: Large kitchen, Butler's pantry, Second kitchen, Cellars, etc.
Good gardens and lawn with two water closets. Coach-house and two-stall stable wholly detached, with Groom's dwelling-room and loft above.

NELLIE BOWMAN AS OLIVER TWIST. *The part was customarily played by women. Mrs Keeley was the first to do so, Sybil Thorndike one of many who succeeded her.*

CHINA COLLECTABLES. *Featuring Dickensian characters of the early novels,* Oliver Twist *and* The Pickwick Papers.

LINCOLN'S INN *(left), the archway leading into the fields.*

FANNY DICKENS (1810–1848). *As children, Fanny and Charles were playmates. They sang comic songs together, and later she would accompany him on the piano. In 1823, when Charles began work at the Blacking Warehouse, Fanny entered the Royal Academy of Music as a pupil, and in 1824 won the Academy's silver medal. In 1835 she sang at public concerts and through her musical work met Henry Burnett, whom she married in 1837. They later moved to Manchester where they came to hold increasingly strict religious views. As a result they gave up all professional theatrical work. For many years Fanny suffered from persistent ill-health. Tuberculosis was eventually diagnosed, from which she died in 1848. Her crippled son, Harry, who possibly inspired Paul Dombey, died one year later.*

PAUL GOES HOME *for the holidays. "But there was much, soon afterwards, which Paul could only recollect confusedly. As, why he lay in bed."*

Dickens rented this house from December 1839 to November 1851. During this time he made several lengthy trips abroad. He made a six-month tour of the United States in 1842, was in Italy from July 1844 to June 1845, and in Switzerland and France from June 1846 to February 1847. During these absences the house was let furnished. This meant that Devonshire Terrace was not always available. For example, before the family set out for Italy, they were obliged to leave Devonshire Terrace and stay at 9 Osnaburgh Terrace for a week or two. Again in February 1847, when young Charley caught scarlet fever and the family cut short their stay in Paris to be near him in London, they had to rent 3 Chester Place for three months.

During his American trips Dickens stayed in hotels. In Italy, he rented accommodation for fairly lengthy periods, first in Albaro, a suburb of Genoa, and then in Genoa itself. The Albaro villa was named Bagnerello after its proprietor but was known to Dickens as "the Pink Jail".

The sala [he explained] goes up sheer to the top of the house; the ceiling being conical and the little bedrooms built round the spring of the arch . . . we have abundance of room.

48 DOUGHTY STREET, LONDON, *where Dickens lived from April 1837 until the end of 1839. Here he completed his first three novels. His daughters, Mamie and Katie, were born in this house, and here his sister-in-law, Mary Hogarth, died.*

MARY HOGARTH (1819–1837) *(top), Catherine Dickens's sister. Mary came to live with the newly married couple in Furnival's Inn and then in Doughty Street. She was a pretty and vivacious girl, of whom Dickens was extremely fond. Her sudden and early death came as a great shock to Dickens, and her memory haunted him for many years. His eldest daughter was named after her.*

THE DICKENS CHILDREN, BY DANIEL MACLISE *(bottom). This picture shows Charley in the centre holding a glass of wine. On his left is Mamie, also with a wine-glass. Katey is looking at Strutt's* Antiquities of England, *while baby Walter, wearing a huge hat, looks on. Behind them is Grip the Raven.*

RESTORATION HOUSE, *where Charles II stayed on his Restoration. It appears in* Great Expectations *as Satis House.*

THE FALSE BOOK-BACKS IN DICKENS'S STUDY. *The door of the Gad's Hill library was disguised as a glazed bookcase. The titles of the dummy book-backs within had been invented by Dickens; for example,* Cat's Lives *(nine volumes),* History of a Short Chancery Suit *(twenty-one volumes), and* The Wisdom of our Ancestors *(Volume 1, Ignorance; Volume 2, Superstition; Volume 3, The Block; Volume 4, The Stake; Volume 5, The Rack; Volume 6, Dirt; Volume 7, Disease).*

Here the family stayed from July to October 1844, and here Dickens wrote *The Chimes.* They then moved to the magnificent Palazzo Peschiere, described by Dickens as follows:

In the centre the grand sala, fifty feet high, of an area larger than the dining-room of the Academy, and painted, walls and ceiling with frescoes three hundred years old . . . Adjoining the sala right and left, are the two best bedrooms, in size and shape like those at Windsor Castle but greatly higher . . .

In these splendid surroundings the Dickenses remained until January 1845, when they set off on a tour of Italy. They then returned to Genoa for the last couple of months of their Italian stay before leaving for home in June.

The next year, Dickens again decided to take the family abroad. This time they went to Switzerland and rented the Villa Rosemont, near Lausanne. It was in a delightful setting.

It cannot be praised too highly, or reported too beautiful [wrote Dickens] . . . there are the hills to climb up, leading to the great heights above the town; or to stagger down, leading to the lake. There is every possible variety of deep green lanes, vineyard, cornfield, pasture-land and wood . . . From a fine long broad balcony on which the windows of my little study on the first floor open, the lake is seen to wonderful advantage . . . Under the balcony is a stone colonnade, on which the six French windows of the drawing-room open . . . One of these drawing-rooms is furnished (like a French hotel) with red velvet, and another with green; in both, plenty of mirrors and nice white muslin curtains; and for the larger one in cold weather there is a carpet, the floor being bare now, but inlaid in squares of different-coloured woods . . .

When they left Lausanne, they took five days to reach Paris.

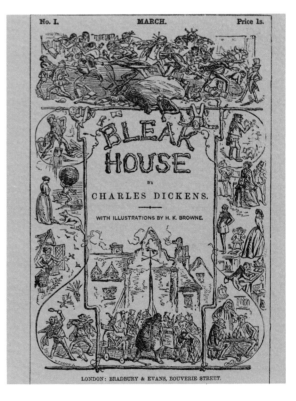

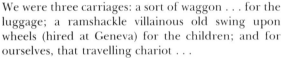

MIGGS RETURNS TO THE
VARDENS. *Having deserted them
during the riots, she comes back.
But Mrs Varden is adamant:
"Let her leave the house this
moment."*

THE WOODEN MIDSHIPMAN.
*This example is on display in the
Dickens House Museum, but
many nautical instrument makers
had a similar sign.*

We were three carriages: a sort of waggon . . . for the
luggage; a ramshackle villainous old swing upon
wheels (hired at Geneva) for the children; and for
ourselves, that travelling chariot . . .

Arriving in a very cold November, they
stayed for a week at the Hotel Brighton,
before moving to 48 rue de Courcelles,
which Dickens rented from the Marquis de
Catellane.

We are lodged at last [he reported] in the most
preposterous house in the world . . . The bedrooms
are like opera boxes, the dressing-rooms, staircases,
and passages, quite inexplicable. The dining-room is
a sort of cavern, painted (ceiling and all) to represent
a Grove . . .

As mentioned above, they returned from
Paris prematurely, and after a holiday in
Brighton, stayed from June to September at
the Albion Hotel, Broadstairs. During the
next few years Dickens was frequently at
Broadstairs, staying either at the Albion or
at Fort House. In 1849 they tried Bon-
church as a place in which to spend their
holidays but tired of it and came back to
Broadstairs. Although Dickens made a trip
to France with Maclise in June 1850, it was

not until 1852 that he began to think
seriously of taking lengthy holidays abroad
again.

Meanwhile, in November 1851, the family had moved into Tavistock House, whose
high railings and gates kept the noisy Ger-
man bands (which Dickens detested) at a
reasonable distance. It was a splendid
house. The drawing-room could accommodate 300 guests and the schoolroom could
be transformed into "The Smallest Theatre
in London" for the benefit of Dickens's
theatrical company. Dickens's study opened
onto a passage running the length of the
house, which allowed him to pace up and

DEVONSHIRE TERRACE,
LONDON, *which Dickens rented
from December 1839 to
November 1851. However, he
had lengthy absences when he was
in America, Italy and
Switzerland. During his tenancy
he wrote* The Old Curiosity
Shop, Barnaby Rudge,
Martin Chuzzlewit, A
Christmas Carol, Pictures
from Italy, Dombey and Son,
and David Copperfield.

TAVISTOCK HOUSE, LONDON. *In 1851 Dickens acquired the lease of this mansion from his friend, Frank Stone ARA. While here, he wrote* Bleak House, Hard Times, Little Dorrit *and* A Tale of Two Cities. *He converted the large schoolroom into "The Smallest Theatre in the World" in which* The Lighthouse, The Frozen Deep, *and the children's plays* William Tell, Tom Thumb *and* Fortunio and his Seven Gifted Servants *were performed.*

CHARLES DICKENS, 1861, *caught in a thoughtful mood by the photographer G Watkins.*

down while he cogitated. Another door was disguised as a bookcase, the dummy book-backs bearing humorous titles such as *The Gunpowder Magazine; Steele. By the Author of "Ion"* and many more.

In 1852, Dickens, his wife and sister-in-law Georgina went for a short stay in Boulogne to see whether it would suit them for a holiday. In June the next year, Dickens wrote to his assistant editor:

I have signed, sealed, and delivered a contract for a house ... which is not a large one, but stands in the middle of a great garden, with what the landlord calls a "forest" at the back ... A queer, odd, French place, but extremely well-supplied with all table and other conveniences ...

This was the Château des Moulineaux, owned by a Monsieur Beaucourt. From June to October the following year, Dickens took another house in Boulogne. This was the Villa du Camp de Droite, which stood not far from the column erected to com-memorate Napoleon's invasion prepara-tions. On 22 June 1854, Dickens wrote to Miss Coutts:

You cannot think what a delightful cottage we have got. The rooms are larger than those in the old house, and there are more of them ... We have a field behind the house, with a road of our own to the Column ... and all for five guineas a week.

In July 1855 the Dickens family went to Folkestone. Dickens had described Broad-stairs in his essay *Our English Watering Place*, and Boulogne in a similar essay *Our French Watering Place*. In the essay *Out of Town* he now described Folkestone (or "Pavilion-stone", as he called it) and himself "sitting, on a bright September morning, among his books and papers at an open window on the cliff overhanging the sea-beach".

Leaving Folkestone in October, the fami-ly crossed to Boulogne, where Dickens and his sister-in-law went on to Paris to find suitable lodgings for a winter stay. Even-tually they took 49 Avenue des Champs Élysées. Finding it was very dirty and smel-ly, Dickens made the proprietor clean it and provide new carpets. He reported back that there was "excellent stowage for the whole family, including a capital dressing-room ... and a really slap-up kitchen". They stayed there until May 1856, when they returned to England.

Almost at once, however, they were off to the Continent again. Once again they were accommodated in Monsieur Beaucourt's property, the Villa des Moulineaux at Boulogne, and remained there until September. It may be noted in passing that Beaucourt was to go bankrupt and move to Condette nearby. Here he owned a chalet which he later let to Dickens as a quiet place where the author could stay with Ellen Ternan. The next year, 1857, Dickens acquired Gad's Hill Place, the first property he ever owned. This was the country house that he had coveted ever since his childhood in nearby Chatham. He could act the country gentleman, walk the lanes with his large dogs, and take visitors on drives to Rochester and Canterbury.

This was the year he met Ellen Ternan, the young actress with whom he fell in love. The next year he and Catherine separated. From this time on, Dickens led a secretive life. Under the name of Charles Tringham he first rented a cottage in Church Street, Slough, and then Windsor Lodge, in Linden Grove, Peckham, where he could meet Ellen. He also took her abroad to Condette and possibly to Paris.

In October 1862 he once again took a house in Paris for his daughter and her aunt. He wrote:

We have a most elegant little apartment here; the lively street in front, and a splendid courtyard of great private hotels behind, between us and the Champs Élysées. I have never seen anything in Paris so pretty, airy, and light. But house rent is fearfully and wonderfully dear.

GAD'S HILL PLACE, *Higham-by-Rochester, Kent, Dickens's dreamhouse. His brother built a tunnel beneath the road leading to the 'Wilderness' where stood the Swiss chalet, a present from the actor, Fechter. Left, Dickens reading to his daughters in the garden of Gad's Hill Place.*

DICKENS *etched shortly before his death in 1870.*

DICKENS'S DESK AND CHAIR. *As this desk was being moved after Dickens's death, some old and torn papers fell out. Did they contain important clues for the solution to* The Mystery of Edwin Drood? *Sadly, no. They were Harry Dickens's shorthand notes for a speech at the cricket club's dinner, and rough sketches of some of the cricketers.*

To complete the record of his homes, mention must be made of the London houses that he took in the latter years of his life so that his unmarried daughter might enjoy the London season. They were all houses around Hyde Park, the last one being 5 Hyde Park Place, which he occupied from January to May 1870. He returned to Gad's Hill Place on 3rd June a sick man, lame in one foot and having difficulty at times with his sight. He was anxious to get on with his latest novel, *The Mystery of Edwin Drood*, but six days after his return he died. For a man who travelled so constantly – and it has not been possible to recount here all the journeys that he made – it is indeed a matter of wonder that he breathed his last in the one house he regarded as home.

The Pickwick Papers
Oliver Twist
Nicholas Nickleby
The Old Curiosity Shop
and
Barnaby Rudge

EARLY NOVELS

The stories and sketches which appeared in *The Monthly Magazine* and other journals between 1833 and 1836 were collected and published as *Sketches by Boz*. When in February 1836 the firm of Chapman and Hall were planning to issue a series of sporting prints by Robert Seymour and needed a writer to compose the letter-press, they decided to invite Boz to do so. Mr Hall called in person at Furnival's Inn. Dickens was delighted to accept and, although he realised that the work would be "no joke", the monthly payment of £14 would be more than welcome. He promptly "thought of Mr Pickwick", and the first monthly part, price one shilling, appeared in green covers on 31 March.

The sales of the first number were modest. The printer bound up only 400 copies. It was not until Sam Weller was introduced in Chapter 10 that the public awoke to the fact that a new comic genius had arrived. Sales shot up and remained high. The concluding number sold 40,000 copies.

Pickwick became the talk of the town. Learned judges quoted it from the Bench. Jealous scribblers hastily produced a variety of plagiarisms – *Pickwick Abroad, Posthumous Notes of the Pickwickian Club, The Pickwick Treasury of Wit, The Pickwick Comic Almanack, Sam Weller's Pickwick Jest Book* and many more. Retailers also jumped on the bandwagon and offered for sale Pickwick hats, Pickwick coats, Sam Weller corduroys, Pickwick cigars and even a Boz cabriolet.

It is not difficult to understand the appeal of *The Pickwick Papers*. The narrative breathed joviality, generosity and goodness

of heart. Mr Pickwick was the innocent steered through a world of rogues and sharks by his comic, worldly-wise servant. Dickens no doubt intended Mr Pickwick to be a butt for practical jokes but as G.K. Chesterton observed:

Dickens discovered as he went on how fitted the fat old man was to rescue ladies, to defy tyrants, to dance, to leap, to experiment with life, to be a *deus ex machina* and even a knight errant . . . Dickens went into the Pickwick Club to scoff, and Dickens remained to pray.

The England of *The Pickwick Papers* was the England of galleried inns, post-chaises, turnpikes, stage-coaches and coachmen,

BARNABY RUDGE AND GRIP, *far left. A fantastic youth with his constant companion, a raven, a very knowing bird.*

MR WINKLE ON THE ICE, *left. "Stop, Sam, stop!" said Mr Winkle, trembling violently, and clutching hold of Sam's arms with the grasp of a drowning man.*

SKETCHES BY BOZ. *This cover of Dickens's first book depicts scenes from some of the sketches.*

SAM WELLER *at the Bath Footmen's Swarry. "When the punch was about half gone, Sam ordered some oysters from the greengrocer's shop; and the effect of both was so extremely exhilarating that Mr Tuckle, dressed out with the cocked hat and stick, danced the frog hornpipe among the shells on the table."*

ostlers, grooms and farriers. It has become the Dickensian England as portrayed on Christmas cards and calendars, a lost fairyland for which we secretly yearn.

For Dickens, though, it was the world of hard fact. As a youthful reporter he had spent some years dashing up and down the country. He knew all about coaching inns. He had actually stayed at those he described: the Great White Horse at Ipswich, the Bull at Rochester, the Angel at Bury St

Edmunds, the Black Boy at Chelmsford, and many others. Like the Pickwickians he was always on the move, and would continue to be. He well knew that the world about him was no fairyland. Talking of his experiences later, he said:

I have been, in my time, belated on miry by-roads towards the small hours, forty or fifty miles from London, in a wheel-less carriage, with exhausted horses and drunken post-boys . . .

The following letter to his friend, Tom Beard, offers a glimpse of the sort of adventures which befell him. This was in 1835, when he set out to cover a by-election.

Yesterday I had to start at 8 o'clock for Braintree; . . . and being unable to get a saddle horse, I actually ventured on a gig. . . . I wish to God you could have seen me tooling in and out of the banners, drums, conservative emblems, horsemen, and go-carts with which every little green was filled. . . . Every time the horse heard a drum he bounded into the hedge on the left side of the road, and every time I got him out of that, he bounded into the hedge on the right side. When he *did* go, however, he went along admirably.

Naturally he drew on such experiences – and earlier ones when he was a shorthand writer in Doctors' Commons – when he was writing *The Pickwick Papers*. The behaviour of his horse on the ride from Braintree is very similar to that of Mr Winkle's on the way to Dingley Dell. Also, the pursuit of Jingle by Mr Pickwick and Mr Wardle is clearly based on those occasions when rival journalists raced their news back to London and possibly bribed ostlers and post-boys:

The boys were sleeping with such mysterious soundness that it took five minutes a-piece to wake them.

His experiences at Doctors' Commons also came in useful when he described what happened when Mr Jingle reached London and took rooms at the White Hart Inn, Borough High Street. Having run away with the supposed heiress, he wished to marry her. So he enquired the way to Doctors' Commons, and was directed there by the Boots, Sam Weller:

Paul's churchyard, sir: low archway on the carriage-side, bookseller's at one corner, hotel on the other, and two porters in the middle as touts for licences . . . Two coves in white aprons – touches their hats wen you walk in – "Licence, sir, licence?" Queer sort, them, and their mas'rs too, sir – Old Bailey Proctors – and no mistake.

When he was only seventeen Dickens had set up as a freelance shorthand writer in Doctors' Commons, renting a little office in 5 Bell Yard. He later described how, on first entering these sleepy courts, he had come across "an old gentleman, whom, if I had seen him in an aviary, I should certainly have taken for an owl, but who, I learned, was the presiding judge". In 1857, Doctors' Commons was abolished. Its functions were taken over by the Divorce, Probate and Admiralty Division of the High Court, and its quiet cluster of old buildings demolished.

Dickens must have found it a change when he entered the Reporters' Gallery of the House of Commons, and an even greater change when he was sent out to cover the rumbustious elections of those days. Inevitably this experience had to be used, and the Pickwickians were duly posted off to Eatanswill into the hurly-burly of the contest between Buffs and Blues. It is not entirely clear in which year this election was supposed to have taken place. In his opening chapter Dickens stated that *The Pickwick*

FARRINGDON STREET *and the Fleet Prison.* "They passed through the inner gate . . . the key was turned after them; and Mr Pickwick found himself within a debtors' prison." *From an engraving, by T. Barber c. 1850.*

COLOUR PICTURE BY ROBERT SEYMOUR. *The landsmen in this picture could almost be Pickwickians, with Mr Pickwick himself giving instructions from the boat to Messrs Winkle and Snodgrass as they descend the rope-ladder. With the wind blowing so strongly, and the sea not at all calm, disaster seems imminent. (By courtesy of the National Maritime Museum.)*

THE POSTHUMOUS PAPERS
OF THE PICKWICK CLUB

Samuel Pickwick sets out on a tour of England with his fellow members of the Pickwick Club: Mr Winkle, a supposed sportsman; Mr Tupman, a would-be Lothario; and Mr Snodgrass, of poetical pretensions. Having met Alfred Jingle, a strolling actor, they find themselves guests of Mr Wardle at Dingley Dell. There, Tupman proposes to Rachel Wardle, a spinster of doubtful age, but she succumbs instead to Jingle's charms, and elopes with him. Wardle and Pickwick pursue the fugitive couple in a chaise to the White Hart Inn, Southwark, where Sam Weller is the Boots. Jingle deserts the lady on payment of £125 and goes his way. When Mr Pickwick engages Sam as his servant, he gives his landlady Mrs Bardell the impression that he is proposing to her. Pickwick's friends arrive to find their leader holding the swooning lady in his arms. This incident leads to the breach of promise case in which Mr Pickwick fails to gain the verdict but refuses to pay the damages awarded to Mrs Bardell. As a result, Mr Pickwick is arrested and imprisoned in the Fleet Prison.

Prior to this, the Pickwickians have had various adventures: witnessing a rowdy parliamentary election, attending a fancy-dress déjeuner, etc. In one incident, they are tricked into believing that Jingle is planning to elope with a pupil at a boarding school, and Mr Pickwick is discovered at midnight, in the school garden, where he had hidden in an attempt to thwart Jingle's plan.

Visiting the poor side of the Fleet, Mr Pickwick finds Jingle in very distressed circumstances. Filled with compassion for the rogue, he gives him money. Then, when Mrs Bardell herself is arrested, for having failed to clear her legal debts, Mr Pickwick decides to pay the damages and thus obtain his own and Mrs Bardell's release simultaneously. In the final chapters, the principal characters are happily married and Mr Pickwick retires to Dulwich.

Papers was set in 1827, but he forgot this very shortly afterwards when he made Jingle describe the 1830 revolution in Paris. Although the great Reform Act had been passed in 1832 abolishing some of the grosser anomalies of the electoral system, it did not introduce the secret ballot; bribery, victimisation and disorder therefore went on much as they always had done. Thus it matters little whether we take the Eatanswill Election as occurring in 1827 or 1836.

Besides covering elections, Dickens also covered the day's sensational trials, and none was as sensational as that of Lord Melbourne, the Prime Minister, who was accused by George Norton of having had criminal connections with his wife, Caroline, a reigning beauty and the granddaughter of Richard Brinsley Sheridan. The prosecution's case depended on three notes allegedly sent to the lady by the Prime Minister. They were as follows: "I will call about quarter-past four, Yours Melbourne."; "How are you? I shall not be able to come today. I shall tomorrow."; and "No House today: I will call after the levee. If you wish it later, I will let you know."

Here was material for a farcical scene too good to lose. In the proceedings in the case of Bardell versus Pickwick, Serjeant Buzfuz accordingly produced the notes reading: "Dear Mrs B. – Chops and Tomato sauce. Yours Pickwick." and "I shall not be home tomorrow. Slow coach. Don't trouble yourself with the warming-pan."

The difference between the two trials was that Melbourne was acquitted while Mr Pickwick was ordered to pay excessive damages. Refusing to do so, he was committed to the Fleet Prison. Debtors' prisons figure largely in Dickens's works, and more will be said about them in later chapters. In *The Pickwick Papers* Dickens directed his fiercest and most direct attack upon them. By the time he came to write *David Copperfield* and *Little Dorrit*, the worst abuses were over and the Marshalsea Prison, where his father had been held, was already being demolished. Mr Pickwick, of course, was sent to the Fleet, which was situated in Farringdon Street, but the scenes Dickens described there were little different from his later descriptions of the Marshalsea. In both prisons he found dirt, noise and discomfort, ragged couples with lots of children

making up beds on the bare floor, swaggering vagabonds drinking brandy and playing at all-fours with greasy packs of cards. Mr Pickwick was appalled to see the underground stone vaults of the Fleet and to learn that human beings actually lived in them. He was amazed to find so many spending their time drinking and smoking and apparently enjoying themselves.

"It's quite impossible [he remarked] that they can

THE TRIAL OF MR PICKWICK *for breach of promise. " 'The plaintiff, gentlemen,' said Sergeant Buzfuz, 'is a widow; yes, gentlemen, a widow. The late Mr Bardell, after enjoying for many years the esteem and confidence of his sovereign, as one of the guardians of his royal revenue, glided almost imperceptibly from the world.' At this pathetic description of the decease of Mr Bardell, who had been knocked on the head with a quart-pot in a public-house cellar, the learned sergeant's voice faltered."*

MR WINKLE MOUNTS HIS STEED. *" 'T'other side, sir, if you please,' said the hostler. 'Blowed if the gentleman won't a gettin' up on the wrong side,' whispered a grinning post-boy. Mr Winkle, thus instructed, climbed into his saddle, with about as much difficulty as he would have experienced in getting up the side of a first-rate man-of-war."*

MR PICKWICK MEETS MR JINGLE IN THE FLEET. *"A man was brooding over the dusty fire. Yes; in tattered garments and without a coat; his common calico shirt, yellow and in rags; his hair hanging over his face, his features changed with suffering, and pinched with famine, there sat Mr Alfred Jingle. 'Gone, my dear sir – last coat – can't help it. Lived on a pair of boots – whole fortnight. Silk umbrella – ivory handle – week – fact – honour – ask Job – knows it.'"*

POSTER *for the 1912 film version of* The Pickwick Papers, *produced by the Vitagraph Corporation, one of the earliest pre-war American film companies.*

mind it much. It strikes me that imprisonment for debt is scarcely any punishment at all."

To which Sam Weller replied:

"Ah, that's just the wery thing, sir, *they* don't mind it. It's a regular holiday to them – all porter and skittles. It's the t'other vuns as gets done over with this sort o' thing: them down-hearted fellows as can't svig avay at the beer, nor play at skittles neither: them as vould pay if they could, and gets low by being boxed up."

The success of *The Pickwick Papers* prompted Richard Bentley to invite Dickens to edit his proposed new monthly journal. This was first advertised as *The Wit's Miscellany*, but when this aroused some derisive comment, the title was changed to *Bentley's Miscellany*. This in turn prompted the question: "Why go to the opposite extreme?" However, Dickens accepted the editorial post and also agreed to write a new story for the magazine. This was *Oliver Twist*, the first instalment of which appeared in January 1837. *Oliver Twist* is a noticeable contrast to *The Pickwick Papers*, which even in its darker episodes contains flashes of humour. *Oliver Twist* is not without humour, though much of it comes from the ironic comments of the author. For example, when Mr Sowerberry, the undertaker, admires Mr Bumble's new brass buttons on his uniform, the beadle explains proudly:

"The die is the same as the parochial seal – the Good Samaritan healing the sick and bruised man . . . I put it on, I remember, for the first time, to attend the inquest on that reduced tradesman who died in a doorway at midnight."

Dickens's principal target in the early chapters was the Poor Law Amendment Act of 1834 which had introduced a new system for the administration of "relief". This Act did not establish workhouses for the first time. This had been done by the Workhouses Act of 1722. But it did give work-houses a new importance. The main purpose of the Act was to put an end to the so-called Speenhamland System which enabled magistrates to supplement wages according to the price of a quartern-loaf and the size of an applicant's family. In the short term, the System had certainly prevented the poor from starving but the long-term effects had been little short of catastrophic. Employers had little inducement to pay reasonable wages if these would be supplemented by the overseers, and, as the supplements also depended on the size of a family, there was every incentive to have as large a family as possible. In the southern counties where the system was most widely adopted, few labourers bothered to learn a trade and thereby increase their earnings. Also, with so many people applying for relief, the poor rate increased fourfold between 1782 and 1817. Small farmers, being asked to pay such a crippling rate, found it more profitable to sell their land and become labourers themselves in receipt of relief. Only the wealthier landlords seemed able to survive. Their wage bills now being much lower, they were able to accept the greatly increased poor rate. As for other classes in the community, all were in danger of becoming paupers.

Something had to be done to remedy this state of affairs, hence the Act of 1834, which was deliberately harsh. It placed the administration of the Poor Law under a central body, the Poor Law Commission, which established a rigorous system of control and inspection. Outdoor relief, except to the sick and elderly, was forbidden. The able-bodied unemployed had the choice of entering a workhouse or starving. If a man decided to enter the workhouse (as he would usually do only as the very last resort), he would be separated from his wife and family, all of whom would be expected to survive under the most unattractive conditions. It was no wonder that the workhouses soon became known as "bastilles".

Dickens took the greatest exception to this new law. There are frequent references to it in his works, especially in *Oliver Twist* and *Our Mutual Friend*. He made a caustic comment in *Little Dorrit* on the provision in the Act which utterly forbade the giving of alms. "Mr Nandy," he wrote, "had retired

MR JINGLE. "*He was about the middle height, but the thinness of his body and the length of his legs, gave him the appearance of being much taller. The green coat had been a smart dress in the days of swallow-tails. It was buttoned closely up to his chin, at the imminent hazard of splitting the back.*"

of his own accord to the Workhouse which was appointed by law to be the Good Samaritan of his district (without the twopence, which was bad political economy)." The Good Samaritan, it will be recalled, had not only provided the injured man with shelter but had given him twopence.

THE PICKWICK PAPERS. *A scene from the 1952 screen version of the novel. This British production by Renown featured an all-star cast including James Hayter (Mr Pickwick), Joyce Grenfell (Mrs Leo Hunter) and George Robey (Tony Weller).*

OLIVER TWIST

Oliver Twist is the name given to an illegitimate child whose mother dies after giving birth to him in the workhouse. He is "farmed out" to the stony-hearted Mrs Mann at the branch workhouse. At the age of nine Oliver is apprenticed to Mr Sowerberry, an undertaker, having narrowly avoided the worse fate of becoming a climbing boy for a chimney sweep. Bullied and ill-treated at Sowerberry's, particularly by Noah Claypole, an older boy, Oliver runs away to London where he meets John Dawkins, the "Artful Dodger", who takes him to Fagin's den. When Oliver accompanies Fagin's gang of boys on an expedition, he suddenly realises that the boys are pickpockets and Fagin is a receiver of stolen goods. Oliver is about to run off when Mr Brownlow, whose pockets are being picked, becomes aware of the thieves, and raises the cry 'stop thief'. The other boys manage to escape but Oliver is caught and brought before the magistrate. Fortunately, Mr Brownlow arrives to tell the court that Oliver is innocent. When Oliver collapses from exhaustion, Mr Brownlow takes him home and looks after him. Mr Brownlow later entrusts Oliver with some books to take to a shop, but on the way the boy is recaptured by two of Fagin's accomplices, Nancy and Sikes. Sikes and Toby Crackit use Oliver to help them break into a house, and have him enter through a window. The household is alarmed: Oliver is shot and wounded and the robbers flee. Mrs Maylie, the lady of the house, and her adopted daughter, Rose, take Oliver into their care.

Meanwhile, Oliver's half-brother Monks, whose father had willed his money to the child of his mistress, Agnes Fleming, has been searching for Oliver to prevent him learning about his true background and legacy. Monks manages to trace Oliver to Fagin's den. Nancy overhears a conversation about this and arranges to meet Rose Maylie secretly at London Bridge to warn her of the danger. Noah Claypole follows Nancy and tells Fagin, who in turn informs Sikes that Nancy has betrayed him. In a fit of rage, Sikes murders her and flees. Attempting to avoid capture, he accidentally hangs himself. Fagin is arrested and condemned to death. The story of Oliver's parentage and Monks's villainy is revealed, and Oliver learns that Rose Maylie, who had been born Rose Fleming, is in fact his aunt. The story ends with Rose being happily married, and Oliver being adopted by Mr Brownlow.

Oliver Twist opens with Oliver's birth in the squalid surroundings of the workhouse. The half-starved condition of the inmates is emphasised in innumerable ways. For example, Oliver and two other small boys are locked up in a coal-cellar for "atrociously presuming to be hungry". Sowerberry and Bumble joke about the small size of the paupers' coffins, and Mrs Mann, the matron, appropriates a fair proportion of the seven-pence halfpenny a week allowed for feeding each orphan in her care. When the new Poor Law begins to be applied, and the Board decides to introduce a diet of three meals of thin gruel a day, with an onion twice a week and half a roll on Sundays, we are told:

It was rather expensive at first, in consequence of the increase in the undertaker's bill, and the necessity of taking in the clothes of all the paupers, which fluttered loosely on their wasted, shrunken forms after a week or two's gruel. But the number of workhouse inmates got thin as well as the paupers, and the board were in ecstasies.

This leads to the famous scene when Oliver Twist has the temerity to ask for more, resulting in his expulsion from the workhouse and his forced apprenticeship to a chimney-sweep.

Dickens was at pains to point out how bleak a future faced those workhouse orphans who managed to survive such ill-usage and neglect. They had little choice in the matter of employment. They were destined either to go to sea, be made virtual slaves in some factory or mine or, as in Oliver's case, be apprenticed to some brutal and callous employer. It is significant that the job with the undertaker, despite the starvation diet and the bullying, is shown to have been infinitely preferable to the job of climbing-boy. Dickens was not only advancing his plot and making his story more exciting when he described Oliver absconding to London and meeting with the Artful Dodger, he was pointing out that the lack of care shown to workhouse children was the reason why so many of them embarked on a life of crime.

Dickens was severely criticised for introducing criminals and prostitutes into this novel. As he wrote in the Preface:

It is, it seems, a very coarse and shocking circumstance, that some of the characters in these pages are

OLIVER TWIST ASKS FOR MORE. *"Oliver rose from the table, and advancing on the master, basin and spoon in hand, said: somewhat alarmed at his own temerity: 'Please, sir, I want some more.'"*

chosen from the most criminal and degraded of London's population; that Sikes is a thief and Fagin a receiver of stolen goods; that the boys are pickpockets, and the girl is a prostitute.

He went on to argue that, unlike some other popular novelists, he had not romanticised crime.

Here are no canterings on moonlit heaths, no merry-makings in the snuggest of all possible caverns . . . no jack-boots, no crimson coats and ruffles, none of the dash and freedom with which "the road" has been,

STOP THIEF! *"Oliver went like the wind with the crowd after him."*

OLIVER TWIST RECAPTURED *by Nancy and Sikes. "Oliver was walking along thinking how happy and contented he ought to feel, when suddenly he was stopped by having a pair of arms thrown tightly round his neck. 'Thank gracious goodness heavins, I've found you! Come home directly, you cruel boy, come!' 'Why, it's Nancy! exclaimed Oliver. 'What the devil's this?' said a man bursting out of a beer-shop! Young Oliver! Come home to your poor mother, you young dog!' "*

POSTER *for the 1948 film version of* Oliver Twist, *produced by The Rank Organisation, directed by David Lean, and starring Alec Guiness as Fagin.*

time out of mind, invested. The cold, wet, shelterless midnight streets of London; the foul and frowsy dens, where vice is closely packed and lacks the room to turn; the haunts of hunger and disease . . . where are the attractions of these things?

Yet some of these things had a strange attraction for Dickens. He spent a lot of time walking those midnight streets, looking into those frowsy dens. The very minds of criminals attracted him. He liked to put himself imaginatively in their place, especially into the place and into the minds of condemned men. He felt and saw all that Fagin felt and saw as he stood in the dock awaiting sentence of death. Already in one of the *Sketches by Boz* he had imagined in convincing detail exactly what a felon must go through in the condemned cell. He would do so again when he came to write *Barnaby Rudge*. Public executions horrified him but he attended the execution of Courvoisier outside Newgate on 6 July 1840 when there was a crowd of some 40,000 onlookers. There was an even greater crowd on 13 November 1849, when he went to see Mr and Mrs Manning hanged outside Horsemonger Lane Gaol. Such were the scenes of unfeeling debauchery that Dickens sent a letter to *The Times* arguing angrily for the end of such spectacles.

On the completion of *Oliver Twist*, Dickens severed his connections with *Bentley's Miscellany*. He and Bentley had been on bad terms for some time. Dickens resented Bentley's interference in what he deemed to be the editor's responsibilities, and when matters did not improve, he resigned. He already had more than enough to occupy him. He had begun *Oliver Twist* while *The*

Pickwick Papers still had several months to run. Then, once *The Pickwick Papers* was concluded, he had agreed to furnish Chapman and Hall with a successor. So, on 31

FAGIN IN THE DEATH CELL. "*He cowered down upon his stone bed, and thought of the past . . . His red hair hung down upon his bloodless face, his beard was torn, and twisted into knots; his eyes shone with a terrible light; his unwashed flesh crackled with the fever that burnt him up.*"

SIKES AND OLIVER. "*Get up*", *said Sikes, trembling with rage, and drew a pistol from his pocket. A scene from the 1948 film, Oliver Twist, starring Robert Newton as Bill Sikes and John Howard Davies as Oliver.*

CHINA PLATE, *showing Oliver amazed at the Dodger's mode of 'going to work'.*

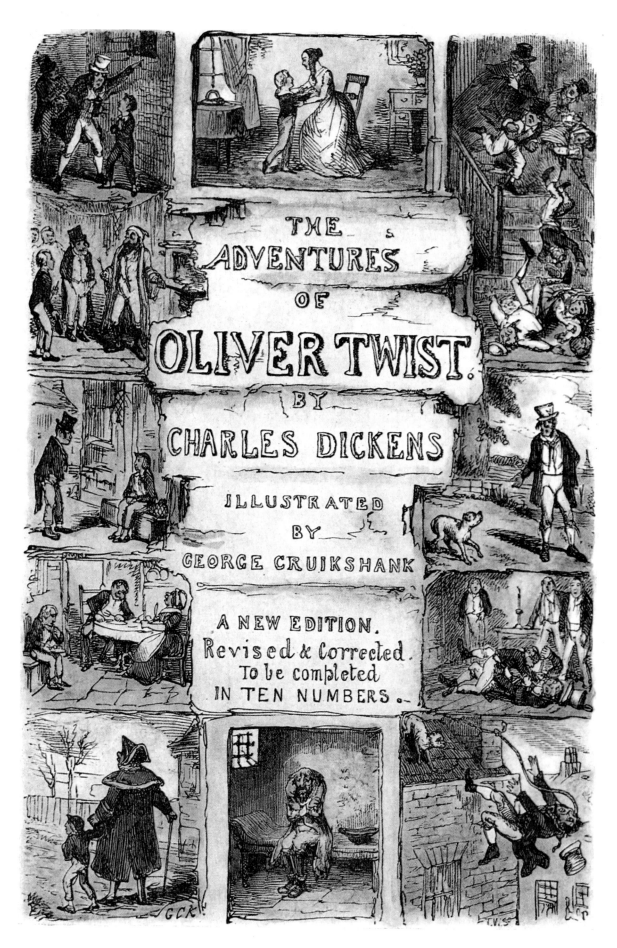

COVER OF OLIVER TWIST *from an edition in ten parts. The cover shows various episodes in the story.*

March 1838, the first part of *Nicholas Nickleby* arrived on the bookstalls.

In the course of its untidy plot, *Nicholas Nickleby* was to glance in many directions, but Dickens's first intention was to expose the notorious schools in North Yorkshire and Durham where unwanted children were farmed out. "No extras, no vacations, and diet unparalleled" was the only truthful, though ambiguous, phrase in their advertisements. So, in January 1838, accompanied by the artist, Hablôt Knight Browne, Dickens set off on a tour of investigation. They stayed at the inn at Greta Bridge before going to Bowes to call on William Shaw at Bowes Academy. It has since been shown that Shaw's school was not the equivalent of Dotheboys Hall, but Dickens certainly borrowed most of his detail from it, while making enquiries about other schools in the neighbourhood. He adopted the stratagem of pretending to be acting on behalf of a widow lady who wished to find a suitable school for her small son. In the course of these enquiries he encountered a

SIR HERBERT BEERBOHM TREE *as Fagin. Tree was a versatile actor who enjoyed playing eccentric parts. His portrayal of Fagin was a great popular success.*

43

NICHOLAS NICKLEBY

After the death of his father, Nicholas and his sister Kate come to London with their mother to ask uncle Ralph for help. Ralph, a moneylender, sends Nicholas off to Yorkshire as assistant to Squeers, a schoolmaster, and has Kate apprenticed to Mrs Mantalini, a milliner. Nicholas finds conditions at the school, Dotheboys Hall, appalling. He befriends Smike, a simpleton whose parents have forgotten him. Smike runs away, is brought back, and is about to be thrashed by Squeers when Nicholas intervenes and beats the schoolmaster. Nicholas and Smike quit the school and go to London together.

Meanwhile, Kate is having difficulties at the Mantalinis. The rascally Sir Mulberry Hawk, aided by his toady, Lord Frederick Verisopht, plans to seduce her. When the Mantalinis' business fails owing to the extravagance of Mr Mantalini, Kate is out of work until she becomes companion to Mrs Wititterly. Nicholas finds employment as an actor with Vincent Crummles and appears at Portsmouth. With Nicholas gone, Sir Mulberry Hawk pursues Kate to the Wititterlys'. Nicholas is called to protect her and overhears Hawk making insolent remarks about her. He demands satisfaction, and being refused, assaults Hawk who is seriously injured. Recovering, Hawk plans revenge on Nicholas through his concern for Smike. Through his connection with Ralph, Hawk arranges for Squeers to capture Smike and hold him prisoner. Nicholas's friends, the Browdies, meet Squeers in London and pretend to be amused at his boasts about Smike's recapture. They go to Squeers's lodgings and manage to set the boy free. Nicholas now enters the counting house of the Cheeryble Brothers, two philanthropists. Ralph and Squeers try to retake Smike by bringing in an alleged father to reclaim him, but their plan fails.

Nicholas has fallen in love with Madeleine Bray, whose father, in the clutches of Ralph, has agreed to see her married to an old miser, Arthur Gride. Madeleine is willing to acquiesce for her father's sake, but Bray's sudden death prevents the marriage. Gride's housekeeper, Peg Sliderskew, absconds with Gride's papers, among them a will leaving a fortune to Madeleine. The will's destruction is prevented just in time. Still intent on revenge, Hawk plans to humiliate Nicholas, but Verisopht refuses to support him. Hawk kills Verisopht in a duel and flees. The downfall of Ralph, Gride, Squeers, and their accomplices inevitably follows, but Smike dies too soon to know that he was Ralph's son, and therefore Nicholas's cousin. Filled with remorse, Ralph hangs himself. The novel concludes with Nicholas marrying Madeleine, and Kate marrying Frank Cheeryble, nephew of the Cheeryble Brothers.

"jovial, ruddy, broad-faced man" to whom he explained his supposed mission.

"Weel, Misther," returned the man, "ar'll spak my moind tiv'ee. Dinnot let the weedur send her little boy to yan o' our school-measthers while there's a harse to hoold in a' Lunnon, or a goothur to lie asleep in." And he warned the lady, fervently: "To keep the lattle boy from a' sike scoundrels."

Nicholas Nickleby resumed the comic picaresque tradition of *The Pickwick Papers* but unlike the latter it is stagey, and heavily melodramatic. Squeers is the comic villain. Having watered the boys' milk to the point where the waiter declares it to be "drownded", he tastes it, smacks his lips, and declares: "Ah! here's richness!" But the other villains are straight out of the early nineteenth-century theatre. At the end of the novel, when Ralph Nickleby prepares to hang himself, a bell begins to toll. "Lie on, with your iron tongue," he soliloquises, "Ring chimes for the coming in of every year that brings this cursed world to its end. No bell or book for me! Throw me on a dunghill, and let me rot there, to infect the air!" Sir Mulberry Hawk is equally a figure out of popular melodrama, attempting to seduce Kate Nickleby and eventually killing the sycophantic Verisopht in a duel. It is quite consistent with the tone of the novel that Nicholas should join Crummles's company of players.

POSTER *for the 1947 film adaptation of* Nicholas Nickleby. *Directed by Cavalcanti, it featured Cyril Fletcher and Fay Compton as the Mantalinis, Sir Cedric Hardwicke as Ralph, Derek Bond as Nicholas, Alfred Drayton and Sybil Thorndike as the Squeers, and Stanley Holloway as Mr Crummles.*

SYBIL THORNDIKE AS MRS SQUEERS *in the 1947 film production, by Heindale Weintraub. Sybil Thorndike was said to have given "a suitably revolting performance" in the role.*

NICHOLAS AND SMIKE *consult in the loft after their daring escape from Dotheboys Hall. A scene from the Royal Shakespeare Company's triumphant and epic stage production in 1980, starring Roger Rees as Nicholas, and David Threlfall as Smike. (Photographed by Chris Davies.)*

Dickens was fascinated by the theatre. He was no mean actor himself and, in a letter to Wilkie Collins, he once declared that he had been a writer as a mere baby but an actor always. On another occasion he expressed the belief that if circumstances had led him in a different direction, he would have been as great a success *on* the boards as he had been *between* them. And indeed, circumstances might easily have led him that way. On leaving school at the age of 15, he was employed until he was about three months short of 17 by Mr Edward Blackmore, a solicitor, who later recalled:

MADAME MANTALINI'S WORK-ROOM, *where Kate Nickleby was set to work sewing, cutting and making-up under the eagle eye of Miss Knag. A scene from the 1947 film version of the novel, starring Sally Anne Howes as Kate Nickleby.*

His taste for theatricals was much promoted by a fellow-clerk named Potter... They took every opportunity, then unknown to me, of going together to a minor theatre, where (I afterwards heard) they not unfrequently engaged in parts.

Mr Blackmore's anxiety to emphasise his ignorance of these activities at the time, underlines the fact that private theatres were notoriously not resorts for respectable people, and certainly not somewhere that anyone wishing to preserve a good reputation would take part on stage. Obviously Dickens was familiar with such theatres and their patrons – the "dirty boys, low copying-clerks in attorneys' offices, capacious-headed youths from city counting-houses ... shop-boys who now and then mistake their masters' money for their own,

TREACLE DAY AT DOTHEBOYS HALL. "'They have the brimstone and treacle,' explained Mrs Squeers, 'partly because if they hadn't something or other in the way of medicine they'd be always ailing and giving a world of trouble, and partly because it spoils their appetites and comes cheaper than breakfast and dinner.'"

46

and a choice miscellany of idle vagabonds" whom he described in the sketch by Boz entitled *Private Theatres*. He doubtless gained this knowledge when he too was a low copying-clerk, and it is most probable that he and his friend Potter were among "the donkeys who were prevailed upon to pay for permission to exhibit" themselves on the stage.

A year or two later, while he was working as a shorthand reporter, he began to study the art of acting seriously. For about three years he attended a theatre almost every night and made a special point of studying Charles Mathews, whom he particularly admired. He practised continually at home, walking in and out, sitting down, standing up, "often four, five, six hours a day; shut up in my own room, or walking about in the fields". He also developed a system for learning parts and, when he considered himself to be ready, he wrote to Bartley, the stage manager at Covent Garden, and asked for an audition. To his delight, he received an invitation to present himself. He at once arranged for his sister, Fanny, to accompany him and play the music for the songs. But when the day for the audition arrived, he was laid up "with a terrible bad cold and an inflammation of the face". So he devoted himself to writing.

Those were poor days for the theatre. The stage was devoted more to what we would term "variety" than to serious drama. In London, only the patent theatres – Drury Lane, Covent Garden and the Haymarket – could present "straight" plays.

All other theatres were obliged to dilute their productions with songs and dance. Thus when he prepared for his audition Dickens had to be ready to sing as well as act. Theatres relied to a great extent on "gimmicks" – child actors, such as Master Betty, equestrian displays, clowns and other diversions more appropriate to the circus. The constant inventiveness of Crummles in utilising all sorts of props – "Real pump! – Splendid tubs! – Great attraction!" – was typical of many actor-managers. Though Dickens exaggerated for humorous effect, he did not depart too far from real life. Thus at Miss Snevellicci's "bespeak" full use had to be made of the pump and tubs, and when at last "Mrs Grudden lighted the blue fire, and all the unemployed members of the company came in and tumbled down in various directions – not because that had anything to do with the plot, but in order to finish off with a tableau – the audience . . . gave vent to . . . a shout of enthusiasm." Neither were Mrs Crummles' talents untypical. She could dance the skipping-rope hornpipe between the acts, and won Mr Crummles's admiration the first time he saw her when she was standing "upon her head on the butt-end of a spear surrounded by blazing fireworks".

Not since Sheridan had there been a British dramatist of any note, and plagiarism was widely practised. There was little exaggeration in the episode where Nicholas Nickleby is set the task of preparing a new play by translating one from the French and making various adaptations to accommodate Crummles's company. Dickens's own works were dramatised and staged without his permission – even before their instalments had been completed – and this remained a constant cause of irritation.

In *Nicholas Nickleby* we can see what most of the dramatic productions of that time consisted of. When Nicholas enters the Green Room he finds:

Here all the people were so much changed that he scarcely knew them. False hair, false colour, false calves, false muscles – they had become different beings. Mr Lenville was a blooming warrior of most exquisite proportions; Mr Crummles, his large face shaded by a profusion of black hair, a Highland outlaw of most majestic bearing; one of the old gentlemen, a gaoler, and the other a venerable patriarch; the comic countryman, a fighting man of great valour relieved by a touch of humour; each of the Master Crummleses a prince in his own right.

MR CRUMMLES REHEARSES A COMBAT. *"At the upper end of the room were a couple of boys, one of them very tall and the other very short, both dressed as sailors – or at least as theatrical sailors – fighting what is called in the play-bills a terrific combat . . . Both were overlooked by a large heavy man, perched against the corner of a table, who emphatically adjured them to strike a little more fire out of the swords."*

Whether the influence of Shakespeare or Walter Scott predominated, it would be hard to say, but the theatre of Mr Crummles was undoubtedly romantic and theatrical. So too were the Crummleses.

"Vincent," said Mrs Crummles, "what is the hour?"
"Five minutes past dinner-time," said Mr Crummles.
Mrs Crummles rang the bell. "Let the mutton and onion-sauce appear."

On completing *Nicholas Nickleby* Dickens felt he needed a respite. For over three years he had been producing a sizeable instalment of fiction every month. In fact, while *Oliver Twist* was appearing he had produced two instalments every month. His thoughts were turning to the possibility of a weekly magazine, written largely by himself, which would bring variety and enable him to indulge his fancy in writing the sort of old-fashioned essays that he had loved as a boy and that Washington Irving was writing in America. He envisaged this magazine being based on the notion of a little club of elderly people who would meet regularly in an old gentleman's parlour where there was a curious old clock. Members of the club would deposit their manuscripts in the clock case, ready to be brought out and read at the

THE CRUMMLES FAMILY. *Another scene from the Royal Shakespeare Company's production of the novel. From left, clockwise, the Infant Phenomenon played by Julie Peasgood, Mrs Crummles (Lila Kaye), Miss Snevellicci (Suzanne Birtish), and Mrs Snevellicci (Thelma Whiteley). (Photographed by Chris Davies.)*

THE OLD CURIOSITY SHOP

Nelly Trent lives in an old curiosity shop owned by her grandfather, a compulsive gambler who firmly believes he will one day make Nell a rich woman, but who has meanwhile become heavily indebted to the dwarf, Quilp. When Quilp realises where his money has gone, he forecloses on the property. Nell decides to take her grandfather away from the temptations of London and they commence a succession of journeys around England. After meeting the Punch-and-Judy men, Codlin and Short, Nell suspects Codlin of planning to disclose their whereabouts to Quilp. She promptly leaves them and, after a short stay with a schoolmaster, goes on to work for Mrs Jarley, who exhibits waxworks. Nell's grandfather is soon tempted to gamble again, stealing Nell's earnings to do so. Once more, she leads him away and they travel through the Black Country, sleeping one night in a foundry, and witnessing a Chartist riot. From there they go north and, meeting their old friend the schoolmaster, find lodgings in a cottage next to an old church.

Meanwhile Quilp tries hard to find them. Dick Swiveller, a friend of Nell, takes employment with Quilp's solicitor, Sampson Brass, and befriends the little slavey whom he nicknames 'the Marchioness'. Dick also lets a room in the Brasses' house to a mysterious 'Single Gentleman' who takes an unusual interest in the whereabouts of the Punch-and-Judy men. By this means he manages to trace Nell to Mrs Jarley's, but no further. At the instigation of Quilp, another friend of Nell named Kit Nubbles is wrongly accused of theft and sent to prison. But the Marchioness has overheard Quilp and the Brasses plotting to incriminate him. Brass is arrested, and Quilp drowns while trying to escape.

At last the Single Gentleman, who is actually Nell's great uncle, succeeds in finding her. Sadly, her health has been so undermined by the hardships she has undergone that she dies before anyone can reach her. Her grandfather is so stricken with grief that he fails to recognise his brother and shortly afterwards he, too, dies.

The book concludes with Sampson Brass being struck off the register of lawyers. Mrs Quilp, after years of misery with her bullying husband, marries again; and Dick Swiveller marries the Marchioness.

next meeting. Dickens thought he might re-introduce Mr Pickwick and Sam Weller, and set out his intention "to take advantage of all passing events; and to vary the form of the papers by throwing them into sketches, essays, tales, adventures, letters from imaginary correspondents, and so forth." He also had a vague idea "when a sufficient quantity of matter in advance should have been prepared", to go to Ireland or America and "write from thence a series of papers descriptive of the places and people" that he would see.

These plans took shape when on Saturday, 4 April 1840, the first number of *Master Humphrey's Clock* appeared. It got off to an excellent start. Around 70,000 copies were sold and an exultant Dickens could write joyfully:

The Clock goes gloriously indeed . . . Thank God for this great hit. I always had a quiet confidence in it, but I never expected *this*, at first.

But his readers were disappointed once they found that the magazine was not to contain a serialised story. Sales fell off. After the fourth number, Thackeray noted: 'Dickens is sadly flat, with his Old Clock.' Dickens, however, was already reconsidering his policy and deciding to discontinue the idea of Master Humphrey and his cro-

nies reading papers in the chimney-corner. In the fourth number he had begun a short story dealing with Master Humphrey's encounter with a little girl. This story was continued in Number 7, and was developed from a short story into a full-length novel, *The Old Curiosity Shop*. It not only halted the decline in the sales of *Master Humphrey's Clock* but became the best-selling of Dickens's novels to date, weekly sales reaching 100,000 before the story was completed.

Being something of an accident, traces of the origin of *The Old Curiosity Shop* can be seen in the first three chapters of *Master Humphrey's Clock*. These are written in the first person, the narrator being Master Humphrey. But once this uninteresting narrator had "for the convenience of the narrative" (as Dickens explained) detached himself from the further course of the story, it was free to move into fresh fields. Dickens introduced Mr and Mrs Quilp in their lodging on Tower Hill, and then a host of other memorable characters – Codlin and Short, Mrs Jarley, Sampson and Sally Brass, and many more. Central to the plot were Little Nell and her grandfather. His gambling mania not only placed him in the clutches of the villainous Quilp but thwarted Nell's every effort to find a place where he would be safe from the lure of the gambling table.

It was the pathetic story of Little Nell which captivated contemporary readers

DICK SWIVELLER *and the small servant.* "To make it seem more real and pleasant, I shall call you the Marchioness."

DICKENS *in 1837 (far left).* "Tell Edward Barrow that I was sitting for my portrait to George Cruikshank when he called today."

DICK SWIVELLER WITH THE SLY DANIEL QUILP. *A scene from the 1974 film,* Mister Quilp, *retitled* The Old Curiosity Shop *by Reader's Digest Films. Among the cast were Anthony Newley, David Hemmings, Michael Hordern and Jill Bennett.*

THE INTERIOR OF THE OLD
CURIOSITY SHOP. "*There were
suits of mail standing like ghosts
in armour here and there,
fantastic carvings brought from
monkish cloisters, rusty weapons
of various kinds, distorted figures
in china and wood and iron and
ivory; tapestry and strange
furniture that might have been
designed in dreams.*"

THE MARCHIONESS. "*I used to
sleep in the kitchen . . . Miss Sally
used to keep the key of the kitchen
door in her pocket, and she
always came down at night to
take away the candle and rake out
the fire. When she had done that,
she left me to go to bed in the
dark, locked the door on the
outside, put the key into her
pocket again, and kept me locked
up till she come down in the
morning – very early I can tell
you – and let me out.*"

and caused many thousands on both sides
of the Atlantic to shed tears on her death.
Yet the book contains some of the funniest
scenes in Dickens. Quilp is indeed "a
hideous dwarf" who treats his poor little
wife abominably and whose mother-in-law,
despite her show of resistance when he is
not present, lives in dread of him. Whenever he appears, however, readers can ex-
pect to be highly amused.

The book is noteworthy for the pictures it
gives of travelling showmen, Punch and
Judy men, exhibitors of performing dogs,
waxworks and suchlike. At the races,

men who had lounged about all night in smock-frocks
and leather leggings came out in silken vests and hats
and plumes, as jugglers or mountebanks; or in
gorgeous liveries as soft-spoken servants at gambling-
booths; or in sturdy yeoman dress as decoys at
unlawful games. Black-eyed gipsy girls, hooded in
showy handkerchiefs, sallied forth to tell fortunes,
and pale slender women with consumptive faces
lingered upon the footsteps of ventriloquists and
conjurors, and counted the sixpences with anxious
eyes long before they were gained . . . The dancing
dogs, the stilts, the little lady and the tall man, and all
the other attractions, with organs out of number and
bands innumerable . . . flourished boldly in the sun.

This passage clearly indicates the close connection between these purveyors of entertainment and petty crime. With its reference to "pale, slender women with consumptive faces" it also hints at the malnutri-
tion and unhealthy living conditions which

must have brought many of these itinerants to an early grave.

Lowly though all these people might be, Dickens realised that there was a hierarchy, a social scale among them. Thus Mrs Jarley regards herself as far superior to Punch and Judy men. "And very sorry I was," she tells Little Nell, "to see you in company with a Punch; a low, practical wulgar wretch." And when Little Nell says how kind they have been, and enquires whether Mrs Jarley knows them, she receives the reply, in a sort of shriek: "Know *them*! . . . Do I look as if I know'd 'em, does the caravan look as if *it* know'd 'em?"

But if Mrs Jarley feels superior to the Punch and Judy men, Miss Monflathers, principal of Miss Monflathers's Boarding and Day Establishment for twenty-six young ladies, feels infinitely superior to Mrs Jarley. Not only that, she tells Nell that she "must be a very wicked little child to be a waxwork child at all . . . when you might have the proud consciousness of assisting, to the extent of your infant powers, the manufactures of your country; of improving your mind by the constant contemplation of the steam engine; and of earning a comfortable and independent subsistence of from two-and-ninepence to three shillings per week."

When one of her teachers begins to quote "How doth the little busy bee", Mrs Monflathers is quick to reprimand her:

"The little busy bee," said Miss Monflathers, drawing herself up, "is applicable only to genteel children. 'In books or work, or healthful play' is quite right as far as they are concerned; and the work means painting on velvet, fancy needlework, or embroidery. In such cases as these," pointing at Nell with her parasol, "and in the case of all poor people's children, we should read it thus:—
    'In work, work, work. In work alway
      Let my first years be past,
      That I may give for ev'ry day
      Some good account at last.'"

Dickens, who never forgot his own experience in the blacking warehouse, was ever keen to place his pen at the service of those who were trying to alleviate the condition of child labourers. Bad as things had been for him, he was well aware that many children suffered much more severely. He had drawn attention to some forms of suffering in *Oliver Twist*. Now he pointed out the evils to be found in those northern and Midland towns where thousands of infants were "assisting" in the manufactures of their country. Some children began to work as young as six years old; many of them would be maimed and crippled in accidents because little care was taken to see that machinery was properly fenced or that infants were properly supervised. Following upon Miss Monflathers's remarks about the proper employment for children of the poor, Dickens directed his story thither:

The paths of coal-ash and huts of staring brick, marked the vicinity of some great manufacturing town; while scattered streets and houses, and smoke from distant furnaces, indicated that they were already in the outskirts. Now, the clustered roofs and piles of buildings trembling with the working of engines and dimly resounding with their shrieks and throbbings; the tall chimneys vomiting forth a black vapour which hung in a dense ill-favoured cloud above the house-tops and filled the air with gloom; the clank of hammers beating upon iron, the roar of busy streets and noisy crowds . . .

Nell and her grandfather find nowhere to shelter in this great bewildering town until they are befriended by a furnaceman who takes them into the foundry where he

HABLÔT-KNIGHT BROWNE (1815–1882), *whose four illustrations for Dickens's pamphlet,* Sunday Under Three Heads, *showed a certain flair and vigour which recommended him to the author. Browne's pseudonym, "Phiz", was chosen to match Dickens's "Boz". He remained Dickens's principal illustrator until the completion of A Tale of Two Cities.*

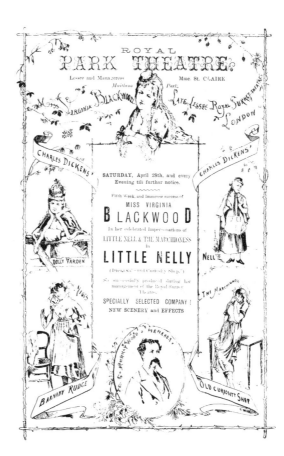

AN EARLY PLAYBILL (*left*) *featuring miss Virginia Blackwood's celebrated impersonations. Miss Blackwood was one of many actresses who impersonated Dickens's characters.*

POSTER *for the 1974 film adaptation* The Old Curiosity Shop. *Like* Oliver *this film was part musical, but not nearly so successful, and it received some poor reviews.*

BARNABY RUDGE

Barnaby Rudge was born the day after the murder of Reuben Haredale, owner of The Warren at Chigwell. His father, the steward, had in fact committed the crime, but this is not revealed until much later in the novel. He had also murdered the gardener, making it appear that the gardener had killed his employer and stolen a cash box. When the gardener's body is found, it is believed to be that of Rudge, who has actually fled. Barnaby was born mentally deficient; his constant companion, Grip the Raven, seems more intelligent.

The story begins 22 years after the crime, in 1775. John Willet, landlord of the Maypole Inn, has a son, Joe, whom he treats like a child. Joe is in love with Dolly Varden, a flirt who trifles with his affections and drives him to enlist in the army, later to be sent to America. A mysterious stranger rides off from the Maypole, then waylays and robs young Edward Chester, who is courting Emma Haredale, niece of the present owner of The Warren, Mr Geoffrey Haredale. This stranger reappears throughout the early part of the novel as he troubles Barnaby's mother to obtain money secretly. At the Maypole is an ostler, Hugh, a wild gypsy-like man, who turns out to be the illegitimate son of Sir John Chester, Edward's father. Sir John has had a bitter quarrel with Mr Haredale, and so opposes any marriage between Edward and Emma.

In 1780, the "No Popery" movement led by Lord George Gordon develops into a riot. Simon Tappertit, apprentice to Gabriel Varden, the locksmith, and in love with Dolly Varden, leads his apprentice "knights" to join the rioters. Hugh and Dennis, the public hangman, also join and then Barnaby is enticed into being the standard-bearer. The rioting spreads: The Warren is burned down, the Maypole is sacked and John Willet is left stupefied. Dolly and Emma are kidnapped. Barnaby is arrested and thrown into Newgate, where he comes across his father. The rioters break into the jail and release all the prisoners, but Barnaby and his father are recaptured. With the sacking of a distillery the rioters destroy themselves and the troops are able to restore order. Dolly and Emma are rescued by Edward and Joe, who has come home from the war minus an arm. The rioters are brought to court. Barnaby is sentenced to death, but is reprieved. His father, Dennis and Hugh, however, are all executed. Simon Tappertit has lost both legs in the disturbances and has to manage on wooden ones. Emma marries Edward, and Dolly marries Joe. Mr Haredale kills John Chester in a duel.

DOLLY VARDEN *and Emma Haredale are rescued. The villain, Gashford is felled by Edward Chester. Emma is clasped by her uncle, and Dolly falls into the arms of her mother and father.*

works. He has come to regard the fire that he tends as a friend, even as a god to whom he can convey his thoughts and feelings. Dickens's description of this workplace is full of fearful similes:

In a large and lofty building, supported by pillars of iron, with great black apertures in the upper walls, open to the external air; echoing to the roof with the beating of hammers and roar of furnaces, mingled with the hissing of red-hot metal plunged in water, and a hundred strange unearthly noises never heard elsewhere; in this gloomy place, moving like demons among the flame and smoke, dimly and fitfully seen, flushed and tormented by burning fires, and wielding great weapons, a faulty blow from any one of which must have cracked some workman's skull, a number of men laboured like giants.

This surely is a description of Hell, with demons moving amid the flames and smoke, tormented by burning fires which rush and roar forth to lick up human souls. Not only did Dickens see Hell in the steel-mills and foundries; he saw it in the town itself and among its people:

Dismantled houses here and there appeared, totter-ing to the earth, propped up by fragments of others that had fallen down, unroofed, windowless, black-ened, desolate, but yet inhabited. Men, women, chil-dren, wan in their looks and ragged in their attire, tended the engines, fed their tributary fires, begged upon the road, or scowled half-naked from the doorless houses ... But night-time in this dreadful spot! – night, when the smoke was changed to fire; when every chimney spurted up its flame; ... when the people near them looked wilder and more savage; when bands of unemployed labourers paraded in the roads, or clustered by torchlight round their leaders.

These vivid scenes come unexpectedly in the middle of a novel which at times has a pastoral quality; for instance, in passages where Nell walks in the churchyard "brushing the dew from the long grass with her feet", or travels by stage-waggon lying "inside that slowly-moving mountain, listen-ing to the tinkling of the horses' bells, the occasional smacking of the carter's whip, the smooth rolling of the great broad wheels, the rattle of the harness" and so on, or in the description of Nell sitting in the little village school, observing as she plies her needle "the hum of conning over les-sons and getting them by heart, the whis-pered jest and stealthy game, and all the noise and drawl of school".

The Old Curiosity Shop is chiefly remem-bered for the death of Little Nell, but it provides a wide panorama of the England of 1840 and includes many of the most comic episodes in all Dickens. Yet some-thing must be said about the death of Nell.

Oscar Wilde said that no-one could read of it without being reduced to laughter. Such a cynical statement is unwarranted. Nell's death was the inevitable consequence of the numerous hardships that she had endured. It was not a contrived episode to wring tears from the eyes of sentimental readers. Surely its inevitability was the reason why Dickens was so distraught at having to describe it. As he was to do on other occasions when his emotions were profoundly involved, he began to write in blank verse:

And now the bell – the bell she had so often heard by night and day, and listened to with solemn pleasure almost as a living voice – rung its remorseless toll for her, so young, so beautiful, so good.

These final words echo the inscription Dickens had composed for the gravestone of his young sister-in-law, Mary Hogarth, who had died in his arms four years earlier:

Young, beautiful and good, God in his mercy numbered her with his angels at the early age of seventeen.

They had been in his mind when he described Oliver Twist's anxiety about Rose Maylie:

"And consider, ma'am," said Oliver . . . "how young and good she is!"

They were to return yet again when he described Florence Dombey taking refuge with Captain Cuttle – "so young, so good, so beautiful". It was no wonder, therefore, that Little Nell's death should remind him of Mary's. He wrote to Forster:

Nobody shall miss her [i.e. Nell] like I shall. It is such a very painful thing to me, that I really cannot express my sorrow. Old wounds bleed afresh . . . Dear Mary died yesterday when I think of this sad story.

The Old Curiosity Shop was followed in *Master Humphrey's Clock* by a novel that Dickens had been contemplating for a long while. In 1836 he had agreed with John Macrone, who had published his *Sketches by Boz*, to write a work of fiction to be entitled *Gabriel Varden, the Locksmith of London*. In view of his monthly commitment to Chapman and Hall and his editorial work for Bentley, this was a most ill-advised agreement, and Dickens soon repented having made it. It would be tedious to relate all the complications which resulted from Dickens having to extricate himself. The end of them all came when Dickens wrote *Barnaby Rudge* for *Master Humphrey's Clock* and the story of Gabriel Varden was merged with that of the idiot boy, Barnaby.

The novel was sub-titled *A Tale of the Riots of 'Eighty'* and, being published in 1840, it dealt with events sixty years earlier. These events were the "No Popery" riots led by Lord George Gordon, a subject which Dickens seems to have chosen for several reasons. It afforded an immediate parallel with Scott's *Waverley*, which had the sub-title *Tis Sixty Years Since*. Although the actual subject-matter was different from *Waverley*'s, it was very similar to that of another of Scott's novels, *The Heart of Midlothian*, which

DOLLY VARDEN, *a portrait by William Powell Frith. Learning that a youthful artist named Frith had made some excellent sketches of some of his heroines, Dickens commissioned him to paint pictures of Dolly Varden and Kate Nickleby. Dickens was delighted with them and brought his wife and sister-in-law to see them in the studio. Frith was greatly impressed when the party arrived in a very dashing curricle with Dickens driving. Later the pictures hung in the dining-room at Gad's Hill Place.*

included the assault on the Tolbooth in Edinburgh during the Porteous Riots. By choosing to write about the Gordon Riots and the storming of Newgate Prison, Dickens was deliberately pitting himself against the acclaimed master-novelist of the century. In addition to this, Dickens wished to make several political points. He saw in the Gordon Riots an example of the sort of disorder which might easily overtake England again if the politicians did not heed the warnings. He had just shown in *The Old Curiosity Shop* how discontent in the manufacturing towns was causing demonstrations by mobs. If such mobs should come together, they would form a far more destructive force that Gordon's undisciplined London rioters.

The town where Little Nell had seen the "maddened men armed with sword and firebrand" was probably meant to be Birmingham. This was where the Birmingham Political Union had been formed, headed by the radical Thomas Attwood, who carried on a continuous agitation for the People's Charter. This famous document, drawn up in 1836 by William Lovett and Francis Place of the London Working Men's Association, was an expression of the deep disappointment felt by the working classes with the Reform Act of 1832. This Act had entirely failed to ensure the representation of the vast majority of the population, and the vote remained restricted to the owners of property. Therefore the Charter demanded universal male suffrage, removal of property qualifications for Members of Parliament, payment of Members, annual elections and a secret ballot. Chartist propaganda was spread by the Leeds newspaper *Northern Star*, owned by the fiery orator, Feargus O'Connor, and throughout the 1840s Chartism was a constant threat to the established order.

Dickens's attitude to it was ambivalent. He sympathised with working-class grievances but feared that their agitation might get out of hand. His two historical novels, *Barnaby Rudge* and *A Tale of Two Cities*, both betray this ambivalent attitude. This is most noticeable in the later novel; in its early chapters he shows great sympathy for the down-trodden French peasantry, and a corresponding detestation of the aristocrats. In the later chapters, however, he expresses

his horror at the revolutionary excesses, and sympathy with every unfortunate who comes before the Tribunal.

In *Barnaby Rudge* Dickens showed no sympathy for the "No Popery" cause. He had no patience at all with the extreme Protestantism of Mrs Varden and her like. Yet he had considerable sympathy with the rioters, regarding them as dupes of scheming rascals. Barnaby himself was typical of many. He was duped into serving under Lord George Gordon. He was then beguiled into carrying the banner and standing on guard while the main body went off pillaging.

In order to put his political message across, Dickens made the little fictitious world of the Maypole Inn stand for England itself. "The Maypole was really an old house, a very old house" and its landlord was John Willet, a "burly, large-headed man with a fat face, which betokened profound obstinacy and slowness of apprehension". Willet stood for the blind conservatism of the English ruling class in 1840. He utterly refused to entertain new ideas. He would not acknowledge that his grown-up son was an adult capable of conducting his own affairs. He utterly failed to see the true character of Hugh the gipsy whom he engaged as ostler and encouraged in many ways. He should not have been surprised when Hugh became a leader of

SECRET MEETING *of the 'prentice knights. "Mr Tappertit mounted a large table, whereon a chair of state, cheerfully ornamented with a couple of skulls, was placed ready."*

STATUETTE OF DOLLY VARDEN *with Joe Willet.*

"HE STOLE UPSTAIRS *to the top of the house, and coming out upon the roof sat down, with his face towards the east.*"

SMITHFIELD, *where Barnaby Rudge helped rid his father of his prison irons. From an engraving by T. Barber, c. 1850.*

the rioters and directed them to attack the Maypole itself:

Here was the bar – the bar that the boldest never entered without special invitation – crammed with men, clubs, sticks, torches, pistols . . . breaking, pulling down, and tearing up . . . some yelling, some singing, some fighting, some breaking glass and crockery.

And Hugh "was the loudest, wildest, most destructive villain there".

Barnaby Rudge has not been appreciated as much as it deserves. It is the best constructed of Dickens's early novels, which is not to imply that it is without faults. It opens with an intriguing scene at the Maypole, the introduction of a mysterious stranger and the recounting of a tale of murder. Dickens had expected his readers to be baffled by the identity of the stranger, and was none too pleased when Edgar Alan Poe wrote to say that he had read the first few numbers and foretold precisely how the plot would unfold. The main business of the novel – the riots – is slow in being introduced and, until it is, the novel does not gather momentum. This is, perhaps, the main criticism to be made.

Barnaby Rudge is quite rich in character and humour. Mrs Varden and her maid, Miggs, provide much of the humour as they chide the honest Gabriel for his late homecoming and his fondness for a drink. The locksmith's apprentice, Sim Tappertit, although at first a farcical figure, provides a link with the rioting when he leads his Prentice Knights to join Lord George. Bar-

naby Rudge, the idiot boy, in his fantastic garb, is an example of trusting innocence, his raven being apparently more knowing and wise in the ways of the world than he is. Lord George Gordon is another example of innocence, having complete reliance on the most villainous and untrustworthy of advisers. The suave and heartless Sir John Chester is obviously modelled on the Lord Chesterfield whose "Letters" to his son are referred to in the book. In the later chapters, Dennis the hangman comes on the scene. His belief that all true Englishmen have a constitutional right to be "worked off" by hanging, rather than by burning at the stake or by some other foreign mode of execution, brings a grotesque humour to the novel.

The reading public did not find *Barnaby Rudge* as appealing as its predecessor. Weekly sales of *Master Humphrey's Clock* dropped from 70,000 to 30,000. Dickens was greatly disappointed. He never lost faith in this novel's merits, and no wonder, for the tremendous descriptions of the rioters bursting into Newgate and burning Langdale's distillery are among the best that he ever wrote.

The financial returns for the entire *Master Humphrey's Clock* enterprise came far short of expectations. It had been a mistake to decide upon illustrating the weekly numbers with woodcuts "dropped into" the text. This proved to be an extremely expensive method, although the result was the most visually attractive of all Dickens's first editions. With profits greatly reduced, so was Dickens's income. This was worrying, for despite his unprecedented success with these first five novels, he was in debt. He owed his publishers some £3,000, largely because of money borrowed to free himself from the agreement with Macrone to write *Barnaby Rudge*, an agreement which had been passed to successive publishers, increasing Dickens's liability. So, although when the final number of *Master Humphrey's Clock* appeared on 4 December 1841, Dickens was the most famous English novelist alive, he was one of the poorest. Rather bitterly, he said in a speech that he did not see "why Fate . . . should not blow out of her trumpet a few notes of a different kind from those with which she had hitherto contented herself".

American Notes
Martin Chuzzlewit
Pictures from Italy
and
The Christmas Books

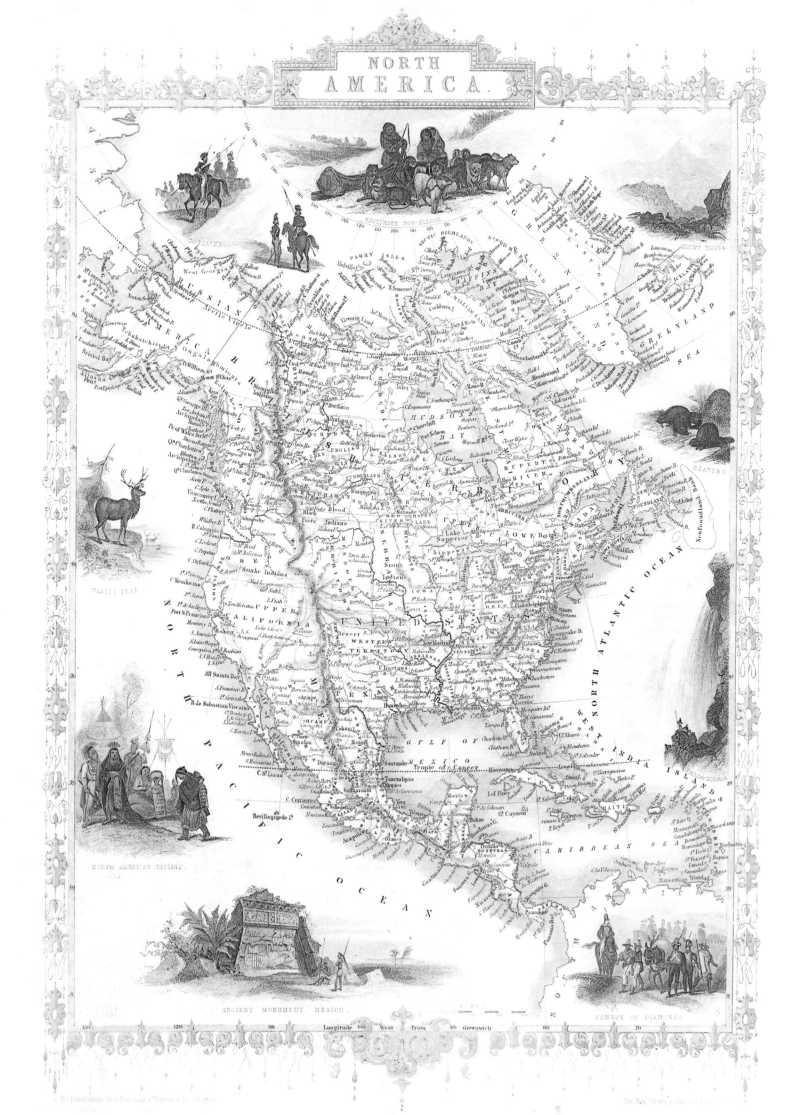

NORTH AMERICA.

ESCHIMAUX DOG-SLEDGE.

COSSACKS.

MOUNT HEKLA.

BEAVERS.

WAPITI DEER.

NORTH AMERICAN INDIANS.

FALLS OF NIAGARA.

ANCIENT MONUMENT, MEXICO.

CONVOY OF DIAMONDS.

Longitude 100 West from 90 Greenwich

CHAPTER
3

INTERIM

Dickens had nursed the idea of visiting America for some years. As already mentioned, it had been among his proposals for obtaining copy for *Master Humphrey's Clock*. Once he had decided to provide his magazine with a continuous serial, however, the proposal had to be shelved. Only when he had completed *Barnaby Rudge* was such a visit possible, and he began to make plans to sail from Liverpool on 4 January 1842. The year 1841 had been an extremely arduous one. Although Dickens was busy with *Barnaby Rudge*, this work was interrupted by a lengthy tour of Scotland from 19 June to 18 July. This must have compelled him to work extra hard whenever he had the time in order to keep up the weekly instalments of his novel. Then, in October, he had fallen ill.

I have been very ill for a week [he wrote to a friend] and last Friday morning was obliged to submit to a cruel operation, and the cutting out, root and branch, of a disease caused by working over much.

The operation, undergone without anaesthetic, was for fistula, and must have been a cruel one indeed. Macready, who called to see Dickens in the evening, confided to his diary that he himself "suffered agonies" merely at learning the details. "I could scarcely bear it," he wrote.

Preparatory to his overseas tour, Dickens applied to insure himself for £5,000. As he told a friend:

If I should get into any danger in my travels, how pleasant it will be to reflect that my darlings are well provided for.

The insurance company, however, was not concerned so much about Dickens's physical health as about his mental state. Some strange rumours had come to the company's ears. In 1837, the publication of both *The Pickwick Papers* and *Oliver Twist* had been suspended for a month. This followed the sudden death of Mary Hogarth, when Dickens had been quite distraught with grief. The interruption was understandable but it gave rise to stories that Boz had been confined to an asylum. A similar story got about in 1840, which his friends did their best to prevent him learning. Unfortunately he happened to see a letter sent to his mother by a relative in Ireland. "What do

MAP OF NORTH AMERICA *by John Tallis, c. 1850 (far left). In 1842, vast areas of North America – Texas and all the West – had yet to be incorporated in the United States.*

AT SEA. *"Steward!" "Sir?" "What is the matter? What do you call this?" "Rather a heavy sea on, sir."*

MODEL OF DICKENS'S
STATEROOM *aboard the*
Britannia *(right). "I shall never
forget the one-fourth serious and
three-fourths comical
astonishment with which . . I
opened the door of, and put my
head into, a 'state-room' on board
the* Britannia *steam-packet . . ."
(By courtesy of the National
Maritime Museum.)*

THE STEAM-PACKET
BRITANNIA. *Commanded by
Captain John Hewitt, the steam-
packet* Britannia, *1200 tons
burden per register, bound for
Halifax and Boston, and
carrying Her Majesty's mails,
sailed from Liverpool on 4
January 1842, and encountered
some of the worst weather for
some years.*

*CENTRAL PARK, NEW YORK,
WINTER, THE SKATING POND.
Published by Currier and Ives,
1852. New York, the city where
Dickens frequently found himself
'skating on thin ice'.*

the papers mean," he read, "by saying that Charles is demented?" John Forster recorded Dickens's "extreme and natural wrath" at these reports. So he was not at all pleased when he found the insurance company being "very particular in requiring an emphatic contradiction of the mad story".

Much of the blame for this must be laid at Dickens's own door. His high spirits often led him into exuberant behaviour. Many of his friends must have wagged their heads over his solemn pretence at having fallen

hopelessly in love with the young Queen, and being heartbroken on learning she was to be married. Two days after the royal wedding he wrote to Forster:

My heart is at Windsor,
My heart isn't here;
My heart is at Windsor
A-following my dear.

And in an extravagant declaration of his state of mind, he continued:

I begin to have thoughts of the Serpentine, of the Regent's Canal, of the razors upstairs, of the chemist's down the street, of poisoning myself at Mrs M—'s table . . . of murdering Chapman and Hall and becoming great in story (SHE must hear something of me then – perhaps sign the warrant: or is that a fable?), of turning Chartist, of heading some bloody assault upon the palace, and saving HER by my single hand . . .

Such letters to his friends must have been talked about. So too must his behaviour at Broadstairs in 1841 when he frightened young Eleanor Picken by threatening to hold her against one of the piles of the jetty until the incoming tide submerged them both. "Let your mind dwell on the column of *The Times*," he told her, "wherein will be vividly described the pathetic fate of the lovely E.P. drowned by Dickens in a fit of

dementia." So if he subsequently had trouble with the insurance company, it was his own fault.

Dickens, his wife and his wife's maid, Anne Brown, sailed from Liverpool aboard the Cunard steamer, *Britannia*, bound for Boston. The crossing proved to be one of the stormiest for years. The passengers were dreadfully seasick, Mrs Dickens and Anne being among the worst sufferers. Then, to cap everything, when the ship arrived off the American coast, it ran aground on a mud-bank. But, on 20 January, they landed at Halifax to a tremendous welcome. It was the same when they reached Boston, and Dickens was left in no doubt about his popularity in the United States. He was invited to dinners and breakfasts, fêted in the theatre, taken to see the sights, while all Boston wanted to shake him by the hand. At New York he found the enthusiasm overwhelming. It was difficult to escape from all sorts of intrusions on his privacy or to avoid hundreds of people shaking his hand. Not surprisingly he developed a violent sore throat and, after a grand dinner held in his honour at the City Hotel, he refused to accept any more invitations. In a letter home, he declared that he was "sick to death of the life I have been leading here".

He must have been sickened, too, by the realisation that, although all these people had read his books and laughed and cried with his characters, the financial rewards accruing to himself were nil. In order to make this trip and have a break of six months, he had received an advance from Chapman and Hall of £1,800. It was paid to him in monthly instalments on which 5% interest was payable. This was in addition to the debt he had already incurred. Hopefully all would be recovered from the proceeds of the next full-length novel that he was committed to write on his return home. But if justice were done, and the American public were to pay him what was justly due, his burden of debt would be quickly lightened. Unfortunately, there was no copyright agreement between Britain and the United States.

Dickens had set sail for America full of idealistic notions about this great new democracy which apparently stood for all the things that he himself stood for – a

society with no hereditary aristocracy, no monarchy, no reverence for birth and breeding, where men were equal, with equal opportunities, where speech was free and liberty could flourish. No sooner did he reach America than he began to be disillusioned. His first disappointment was the American press. Even as the *Britannia* approached the wharf, about a dozen men had leapt aboard "with great bundles of newspapers under their arms". Dickens took them to be newsboys, and was amazed to learn that they were editors. He was also

RICHMOND. *"We drove to the hotel; two or three citizens were balancing themselves on rocking chairs and smoking cigars."*

THE NICKLEBY PORTRAIT, *below. An engraving of the painting by Daniel Maclise which might now be seen in the National Portrait Gallery.*

CATHERINE DICKENS, *left. Dickens praised her for the way she endured discomfort on the trip to America in 1842, and for her acting in the play* A Roland for an Oliver *during their stay in Montreal.*

THE PERKINS INSTITUTION FOR THE BLIND, NEAR BOSTON (*top*). *Here Dickens saw Laura Bridgman, a deaf, dumb, and blind patient.*

DR. SAMUEL G. HOWE (*above*), *Director of the Perkins Institution, whose work with Laura Bridgman greatly impressed Dickens.*

THE ARTIST IN BOOTS: *Dickens orders a new pair from an American bootmaker. "When he had finished, he fell into his old attitude, and taking up my boot again, mused for some time. 'And this,' he said at last, 'is an English boot, is it? This is a London boot, eh?' He mused over it again, after the manner of Hamlet with Yorick's skull."*

disgusted with the contents of these papers. He conveyed this opinion when he described the fictitious newsvendors in *Martin Chuzzlewit*:

"Here's this morning's New York Sewer! Here's this morning's New York Stabber! Here's the New York Family Spy! Here's the New York Private Listener! Here's the New York Peeper! Here's the New York Plunderer! Here's the New York Keyhole Reporter! Here's the New York Rowdy Journal! Here's all the New York papers!"

He was disappointed, too, at discovering (as Martin Chuzzlewit was to discover) that there was an aristocracy in America, composed (as Colonel Diver was to explain) "of intelligence, sir, of intelligence and virtue. And their necessary consequence in this republic, Dollars, sir". Dickens was irritated at being told again and again, whenever he was introduced to someone, that that person was one of the most remarkable men in the country. Eventually he could not refrain from bursting out:

Good God, sir! They are all so! I have scarcely met a man since my arrival who wasn't one of the most remarkable men in the country.

Normally Dickens enjoyed being lionised, but these attentions shown him by the Americans were too much altogether.

If I turn into the street, I am followed by a multitude. If I stay at home, the house becomes with callers like a fair . . . If I go to a party in the evening, I am so inclosed and hemmed about by people . . . that I am exhausted for want of air . . . I take my seat in a railroad car, and the very conductor won't leave me alone. I get out at a station, and can't drink a glass of water without having a hundred people looking down my throat.

As he became more and more irritated by the Americans, so they became more annoyed with him. There were several causes of this friction. There was the question of copyright which Dickens was bold enough to raise at a great banquet in his honour. He told his hearers that if there had been an agreement on this, "Scott might not have sunk beneath the mighty pressure on his brain, but might have lived to add new creatures of his fancy to the crowd which . . . gather round your winter evening hearths". He conjured up a picture of Scott in his last days, "faint, wan, dying, crushed both in mind and body by his honourable struggle" to pay off the debts incurred by the failure of his publishers, while all that he had done to delight millions "brought him not one friendly hand to help to raise him from that sad, sad bed . . . nor one grateful dollar-piece to buy a garland for his grave". This speech caused a sensation. Dickens wrote home:

My friends were paralysed with wonder at such an audacious daring. The notion that I, a man alone by himself, in America, should venture to suggest to the Americans that there was one point on which they were neither just to their own countrymen nor to us, actually struck the boldest dumb . . . I wish you could have seen the faces that I saw, down both sides of the table at Hartford, when I began to talk about Scott. I wish you could have heard how I gave it out. My blood so boiled as I thought of the monstrous injustice that I felt as if I were twelve feet high when I thrust it down their throats.

In a letter he railed at the American press generally:

Is it not a horrible thing that scoundrel-booksellers should grow rich here from publishing books, the

authors of which do not reap one farthing from their issue, by scores of thousands? And that every vile, blackguard, and detestable newspaper, – so filthy and bestial that no honest man would admit one into his house for a water-closet doormat – should be able to publish those same writings, side by side, cheek by jowl, with the coarsest and most obscene companions, with which they *must* become connected in course of time, in people's minds?

It has been argued that Dickens's agitation on behalf of an international copyright agreement, far from procuring it, actually retarded it. It might have been obtained soon after 1842, whereas not until 1891 was such an agreement with Great Britain eventually signed. It has been suggested that Dickens aroused so much support for his case that the American publishers became alarmed at the danger of losing much lucrative business. They speedily assembled a convention of booksellers throughout the United States. A memorial was sent to Congress seeking a duty to be imposed on imported books, supported by statistics to show how much money was involved in the American publishing industry and how much employment depended upn it. They also argued that, if English authors retained control over their own works and could object to their being amended or adapted, American editors would be unable to make

these works suitable for American taste.

Dickens paid many tributes to the generosity, courtesy and kindness which were shown to himself and his wife wherever they went. But, with America generally, he had become sadly disillusioned. America was not the great Republic, the land of liberty, of which he had dreamed.

NEW YORK DANCERS. "*Snapping his fingers, rolling his eyes, turning in his knees, spinning about on his toes and heels.*"

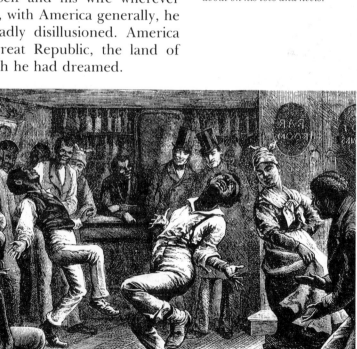

NIAGARA FALLS *"To have Niagara before me, lighted by the sun and by the moon, red in the day's decline; this was enough."*

I don't like the country, [he told John Forster]. I would not live here, on any consideration. It goes against the grain with me. It would with you. I think it impossible, utterly impossible, for any Englishman to live here and be happy. As to the causes, they are too many to enter upon here.

One of these causes – a minor one, no doubt – was the widespread habit of chewing tobacco and spitting. In Washington he visited both houses of Congress and found them both:

handsomely carpeted, but the state to which these carpets are reduced by the universal disregard of the spittoon . . . and the extraordinary improvements on the pattern which are squirted and dabbled upon it in every direction, do not admit of being described . . . I

BOZ IN A-MERRY-KEY. *After Dickens published* American Notes for General Circulation, *which criticised many aspects of American society, there appeared an American riposte entitled* English Notes, intended for Very Extensive Circulation. *Then in London, a comic song,* Yankee Notes for English Circulation, or Boz in A-Merry-Key, *was published with this illustration by Alfred Crowquill.*

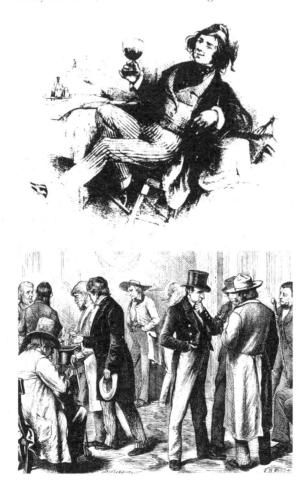

IN THE WHITE HOUSE. *"The President (John Tyler) got up and said: 'Is this Mr Dickens?' – 'Sir', returned Mr Dickens, 'it is.' 'I am astonished to see so young a man, Sir,' said the President. Mr Dickens smiled, and thought of returning the compliment – but he didn't."*

was surprised to observe that even steady old chewers of great experience are not always good marksmen . . . Several gentlemen called upon me, who, in the course of conversation frequently missed the spittoon at five paces.

He was repelled, too, by the Americans' lack of table manners, and the way in which meals were merely occasions for getting food into one's inside as quickly as possible, instead of being times for fellowship and relaxed conversation. Later, in *Martin Chuzzlewit* he described a meal in Mrs Pawkin's lodging-house:

It was a numerous company, eighteen or twenty perhaps . . . All the knives and forks were working away at a rate that was quite alarming; very few words were spoken, and everybody seemed to eat his utmost in self-defence, as if a famine were expected to set in before breakfast-time tomorrow morning . . . The sharpest pickles vanished, whole cucumbers at once, like sugar-plums, and no man winked his eye. Great heaps of indigestible matter melted away as ice before the sun. It was a solemn and awful thing to see.

The widespread violence which was daily reported in the newspapers – shootings and stabbings – was another cause of his revulsion. For example, in Wisconsin, after a heated exchange of words, a member of the legislative council was shot dead on the floor of the chamber by another member. In Iowa,

A Mr Bridgman having had a difficulty with a citizen of the place; Mr Ross – a brother-in-law of the latter, provided himself with one of Colt's revolving pistols, met Mr B. in the street and discharged the contents of five of the barrels into him, each shot taking effect. Mr B. though horribly wounded and dying, returned the fire and killed Ross on the spot.

In Arkansas, a "severe rencontre" between a Mr Loose and a Mr Gillespie led to the latter being slain with a bowie-knife. *The Caddo Gazette* reported the frightful death of Colonel Robert Potter who had been set upon and captured by an enemy named Rose. His captor offered him the chance of saving his life. He was given a head start and told to run. He was also promised immunity until he had covered a certain distance. But Rose and his accomplices soon began to overtake the unfortunate colonel, who in desperation dived into a lake in the hope of saving himself. As his head broke the surface of the water again, it was riddled with gunshot.

Appalling as these things were, Dickens was most appalled by the institution of slavery. When he crossed into the slave state of Virginia, he noted

an air of ruin and decay abroad, which is inseparable from the system . . . There is no look of decent comfort anywhere . . . In the negro car belonging to the train in which we made this journey were a mother and her children who had just been purchased; the husband and father being left behind with their old owner. The children cried the whole way, and the mother was misery's picture. The champion of Life, Liberty, and the Pursuit of Happiness who had bought them, rode in the same train and every time we stopped, got down to see that they were safe.

His attacks on slavery won applause from the Abolitionists, but antagonised many others. Even those who could not support slavery felt he was wrong to interfere in what was an American problem.

Dickens made an extensive tour of the eastern states, visiting a number of prisons, hospitals, factories and other institutions. In New York State he was very interested to see a Shaker village. In Boston he was immediately impressed by the work of Dr Howe at the Perkins Institution for the Blind (see page 62). Dr Howe's patient teaching had enabled a young girl named Laura Bridgman, left blind and deaf through illness and with her sense of taste and smell blunted, to lead a useful and happy life. Dickens took careful note of all that he saw and heard on these visits and, ever the journalist, reported them in lengthy letters addressed to his friend, Forster. They were to form the basis of his next book, *American Notes for General Circulation*.

American Notes was greeted in America with a storm of abuse. Dickens's strictures on the press, on spitting and on slavery lost him several American friends. When Dickens's next novel, *Martin Chuzzlewit*, was published, several others became distinctly cool towards him.

Dickens intended *Martin Chuzzlewit* to demonstrate various aspects of selfishness, and this theme motivated the plot. But at the end of the fifth monthly number, Dickens made Martin Chuzzlewit make the sudden announcement that he would go to America. Readers were then kept in suspense for two months. Then in the seventh number, Martin's first impressions of the United States were revealed. They were

wholly unfavourable and doubly obnoxious to American readers because they were couched in such bitterly satiric terms.

For a comparatively expensive travel book, *American Notes* sold extremely well. Sales of *Martin Chuzzlewit*, on the other hand, proved to be very disappointing. They reached only some 20,000 copies a month compared with *Barnaby Rudge*'s 30,000 and *The Old Curiosity Shop*'s 70,000 to

DICKENS READING *THE CHIMES in Forster's House, 2 December 1844, by Daniel Maclise. Forster declared that Maclise's drawing "will tell the reader all he can wish to know. He will see of whom the party consisted; and may be assured that in the grave attention of Carlyle, the eager interest of Stanfield and Maclise, the keen look of poor Laman Blanchard, Fox's rapt solemnity, Jerrold's skyward gaze, and the tears of Harness and Dyce, the characteristic points of the scene are sufficiently rendered."*

REDLAW AND THE PHANTOM, *by John Leech, from* The Haunted Man. *"As the gloom and shadow thickened behind him . . . it took, by slow degrees . . . an awful likeness to himself." The Phantom's gift of forgetting sorrows, wrongs and troubles is infectious, however. Redlaw finds it blighting the lives of all around him. He begs to lose it, and when it is taken away, he realises the full meaning of the words "LORD KEEP MY MEMORY GREEN".*

MARTIN CHUZZLEWIT

This novel is a study in selfishness. Rich Old Martin Chuzzlewit is surrounded by a host of fawning relatives all hoping to inherit his wealth. He cares only for his grandson, Young Martin, yet the youth is not only as selfish as the others, he has also antagonised his grandfather by wishing to marry Mary Graham, Old Martin's companion. One of the relatives, Pecksniff, an obsequious hypocrite, has taken Young Martin as pupil architect, but at the old man's bidding, summarily dismisses him. Left without support, Martin decides to go to America with Mark Tapley, an irrepressibly cheerful man anxious to test his cheerfulness in adversity. In America they face great hardship, especially in the swampy Eden, where they both catch fever. Reformed by Mark's solicitude for him, Martin nurses his friend back to health.

In England, one of Pecksniff's daughters, the giggly Merry, agrees to marry her cousin Jonas Chuzzlewit in order to spite her sister. She soon regrets it, for Jonas is a cruel brute who has become involved in a bogus insurance company run by another shady character, Montague Tigg. When Jonas's father, Anthony, dies suddenly, Tigg suspects Jonas of having poisoned him. With a view to blackmailing him, Tigg engages a detective to watch Jonas's movements; meanwhile the monthly nurse, Mrs Gamp, discovers that Jonas had purchased poison. Although Jonas had indeed planned to kill his father, he had been prevented from doing so by his father's clerk, Chuffey. The shock of learning of his son's intended villainy had caused the old man to have a heart attack. Finding himself hounded by Tigg, Jonas murders him and hides the body; but to no avail; he is arrested anyway, and poisons himself en route to prison.

Meanwhile, Pecksniff reveals his hypocrisy by making improper advances to Mary Graham. Old Martin forgives his grandson who is thus able to marry her. Tom Pinch, his friend and fellow pupil at Pecksniff's is found employment in London and Old Martin gives further proof of his own unselfishness by providing for Jonas's widow.

100,000. A contributory cause might have been the current financial recession which led to all publishers restricting their output just at that time. More probably, however, Dickens's popularity had declined somewhat. The public had been dissatisfied with *Barnaby Rudge* and, having had a year's break, Dickens had to some extent lost contact with his readers.

The poor sales greatly concerned Chapman and Hall, Dickens's publishers. They had advanced Dickens £1,800, but stipulated in the contract for *Martin Chuzzlewit* that sales would be reviewed after the fifth monthly number. Should it then appear that Dickens's share of profits would be insufficient to repay this advance by the time the book was completed, the publishers would be entitled to deduct an additional £50 each month from the sum payable to Dickens as stipend. They were reluctant to invoke this clause. After all, Dickens had proved a real money-spinner from the publication of *Pickwick* onwards. So Chapman counselled patience. Edward Hall, however, could not agree and decided to remind Dickens of the terms of the agreement. He might have thought he was being tactful but Dickens blew up immediately. Even when the partners attempted to mend

MRS GAMP JOINS DICKENS'S ACTORS. *"If you're a Christian man, show me where to get a second-cladge ticket to Manjester."*

matters and assured him that they had no intention of deducting the £50 a month, Dickens insisted that they should. "I am so irritated, so rubbed in the tenderest part of my eyelids with bay-salt," he wrote furiously to Forster. "I am bent on paying Chapman and Hall down. And when I have done that, Mr Hall shall have a piece of my mind." The result was that, once the monthly instalments of *Martin Chuzzlewit* were completed and his second Christmas book, *The Chimes*, had been published, he broke his connection with Chapman and Hall. He turned to Bradbury and Evans instead.

Although this *contre-temps* put Dickens off writing anything for a few days, he was soon back at work. He felt that *Martin Chuzzlewit* was "in a hundred points immeasurably the best of my stories". He greatly enjoyed writing it. After producing Chapter 21, he wrote to a friend: "I have nearly killed myself laughing at what I have done . . .". And in a letter from Broadstairs to the American professor, Felton, he described himself: "In a bay-window in a one-pair sits, from nine o'clock to one, a gentleman with rather long hair and no neck-cloth who writes and grins as if he thought he were very funny indeed."

This belief in *Martin Chuzzlewit*'s humour has been upheld by readers ever since. The book is one of the funniest Dickens ever wrote. It contains some of his most famous

DR SOUTHWOOD SMITH *published influential reports on the employment of children, on public health, on cholera and yellow fever.*

MR PECKSNIFF CALLS ON OLD MARTIN *(left). "Martin Chuzzlewit wishes you had been hanged, before you had come here to disturb him."*

ST LUKE'S ASYLUM. *Dickens was told about an inmate, an erstwhile telegraph operator. "It is impossible to conceive what delirious messages that man may have been sending."*

characters – Pecksniff, Mrs Gamp, Mrs Todgers, Betsey Prig, Tom Pinch, Mark Tapley and the fraudulent Montague Tigg, who is eventually murdered by the villainous Jonas Chuzzlewit. Time has so changed the American scene that few American readers are now stung by Dickens's criticism. They join in the laughter instead. Thus the novel has become one of the most popular of Dickens's works, selling in its thousands down the years. But when it first appeared its poor reception gave Dickens serious doubts about his ability to remain England's best-selling author.

It is apparent, therefore, that after Dickens returned from America his life entered a new phase. The trip had, inevitably, greatly widened his vision. He had always been interested in social questions, as his earlier novels clearly show. After 1842 he began to involve himself more actively in assisting charities, raising funds for various worthy causes and bringing social problems to the notice of a wider public. He spoke at dinners in aid of institutions such as the Hospital for Consumptives and Diseases of the Chest, of the Aged and Infirm, Deaf and Dumb, and of Dr Southwood Smith's Sanatorium. This latter institution was opposite Dickens's house in Devonshire Terrace. Southwood Smith had been a member of the Children's Employment Commission which had looked into the conditions in which children were employed in mines and factories. When he sent a copy of the Commission's Report across to his neighbour, Dickens read it with appalled interest. He at once wrote to let Smith know that he was "so perfectly stricken down by the blue-book" that he intended to compose a cheap pamphlet entitled *An Appeal to the People of England on behalf of the Poor Man's Child.* Although he never carried out this idea, he did make such an appeal in a different and more telling way.

In the meantime, Dickens exerted himself greatly on behalf of the seven children orphaned by the death of their actor father, Edward Elton, who had been drowned when the ship he was travelling in struck a rock off Holy Island and foundered. Once he learned the situation of the bereaved family, Dickens formed a committee, wrote numerous letters to persons who might help and did all he could for the children, such as getting apprenticeships for the older girls. These were not the only children about whom he was concerned. In order to gain first-hand experience of Ragged Schools, he went along to the one at Saffron Hill – as he expressed it, to take his seat "among the fluttering rags" there. Such interests were bringing him in closer touch with Miss Angela Burdett Coutts, with whom he would soon be working very closely as her adviser and colleague in a number of charitable projects.

Another development during this period was Dickens's interest in mesmerism. Even before going to America he had been initiated into "animal magnetism" (as he termed it) by his friend, Dr John Elliotson. In May 1841 Elliotson had invited him to his house, where he promised to show Dickens "a very

curious and perfectly genuine case of mesmerism". Elliotson had also introduced him to the Reverend Chauncey Hare Townshend, the author of *Facts in Mesmerism*, who gave demonstrations with the assistance of his Belgian "magnetic boy", Alexis. It was claimed that this boy was able, under mesmerism, to see through his forehead and even through the back of his head. "He fails in a crowd," Dickens told Lady Blessington, "but is marvellous before a few." Soon Dickens began to practice mesmerism himself. When he was in Pittsburgh, he tried his skill on his wife. "In six minutes, I magnetised her into hysterics," he reported, "and then into the magnetic sleep. I tried again next night and she fell

CANONBURY TOWER, ISLINGTON. *The district hereabouts features in several of Dickens's works – Oliver Twist, Nicholas Nickleby, and Bleak House.*

MINIATURE FIGURINE OF MRS GAMP.

TOM PINCH INTERCEDES (*far left*) *between the angry Martin Chuzzlewit and Mr Pecksniff, who, stepping hastily back, has fallen in a sitting posture on the ground.*

UNDERGROUND WORKERS (*left*) *by Margaret Gillies, the first illustration to appear in a government Blue Book. Southwood Smith felt that while few MPs and peers would bother to read his report, they would look at the picture.*

PORTRAIT OF DR JOHN ELLIOTSON. *Elliotson was obliged to resign the chair of medicine at University College Hospital, London, following attacks on his use of mesmerism. He demonstrated hypnosis to Dickens, who placed utmost faith in him. "If my own life, or my wife's, or that of either of my children were in peril tomorrow, I would trust it to him, implicitly."*

CHEAPSIDE AND POULTRY. *The very heart of the City of London. Hereabouts was Scrooge's counting-house. Beyond Poultry lay Cornhill where Bob Cratchit went down the slide.*

into the slumber in little more than two minutes." He was to use this skill quite frequently when, a year or two later, he was in Italy; it would lead to trouble between Catherine and himself.

In October 1843, while still only half-way through *Martin Chuzzlewit*, Dickens began to write *A Christmas Carol*. The promise to Southwood Smith to do something for the poor man's child had not been forgotten but the original idea had been entirely changed. Explaining his reasons to Dr Smith, he said:

When you know them, and see what I do, and where, and how, you will certainly feel that a sledge-hammer

has come down with twenty times the force – twenty-thousand times the force – I could exert by following out my first idea.

The plot for the little story evidently matured in his mind throughout the summer. He incorporated in it details he had intended to use in *Martin Chuzzlewit* which he had planned to open on the Cornish coast "in some terribly dreary iron-bound spot", or perhaps "in the lantern of a lighthouse". Both of these scenes were used in "Stave Three" of *A Christmas Carol*.

Dickens allowed himself very little time to write the book and get it published. By dint of "blazing away" at *Martin Chuzzlewit*, "only stopping ten minutes for dinner" some evenings, and "working from morning until night" upon the *Carol*, he managed to complete it before the end of November and see it published on 19 December. It proved to be a wonderful success – "the greatest, I think, I have ever achieved," Dickens declared. As Robert L. Patten has observed: "Into it he poured all his present anxieties and concerns, his perplexities about money, time, gifts (like the Christmas turkey), love, ambition, social injustice, reformation, spiritual conversion, life, death." A second edition was advertised on 6 January in view of unprecedented demand. Financial success seemed assured.

Financial success was, of course, urgently needed. The profits from *Martin Chuzzlewit* were poor. Dickens had voluntarily given up £50 a month, and by doing so had been obliged to borrow from his most intimate friends. A great deal was therefore expected of *A Christmas Carol*. So Dickens had gone to some lengths to ensure its appearing in a most attractive format. The gilt edges to the pages, the cloth covers with the title in gold on the front and spine, and the coloured etchings by Leech made each small volume a delight. They also increased the cost of production.

When Chapman and Hall sent Dickens the accounts, his heart fell. He wrote in anguish:

The first six thousand copies show a profit of £230 . . . I had set my heart and soul upon a Thousand clear. What a wonderful thing it is, that such a great success should occasion me such intolerable anxiety and disappointment! My year's bills, unpaid, are so terrific that all the energy and determination I can possibly exert will be required to clear me . . . I am not afraid, if I reduce my expenses; but if I do not, I shall be ruined . . .

It is difficult to realise that Dickens ever had such financial problems. He had been a best-selling novelist ever since *The Pickwick Papers*, and one of the most prolific. To some extent his very success had caused difficulties. Being inexperienced, he had put his signature to unwise agreements. But he was also burdened with a family which made great demands upon him, and as the years went on these demands increased. Nine of his children survived childhood, and his sons (with one notable exception) all had a tendency to run into debt from which they expected their father to rescue them. His brothers also made demands upon him. So too did his parents. His father regarded him as an inexhaustible fount of ready cash. He had sold odd pages of his son's manuscripts, sent him urgent notes for help when arrested for debt, and even gone wheedling to Chapman and Hall to extract small loans or seek assistance in getting a £5 transit ticket from the Watermen's Company.

It was in vain for Dickens to try and keep his parents well away from him. He placed them in a delightful cottage in Devon but before long they were back in London. At times, his patience with his father gave way

altogether. "He, and all of them," he wrote angrily to his old friend, Tom Mitton, "look upon me as a something to be plucked and torn to pieces for their advantage." For the remainder of his life he was never to be free from what Forster termed "the many never-satisfied, constantly-recurring claims from family quarters, not the more easily avoidable because unreasonable and unjust." So, although Dickens had just published the most famous of his Christmas stories, the one Thackeray described as "a national benefit, and to every man and woman who

VIEW OF BROADSTAIRS. *Dickens and his family spent many holidays at Broadstairs, which he described in his article* Our English Watering Place. *"The ocean lies winking in the sunlight like a drowsy lion – the fishing boats in the tiny harbour are all stranded in the mud . . . In truth, our watering-place itself has been left somewhat high and dry by the tide of years."*

MR PECKSNIFF (*far left*). *"Perhaps there never was a more moral man than Mr Pecksniff especially in his conversation and correspondence . . . He was a most exemplary man; fuller of virtuous precept than a copybook. Some people likened him to a direction-post, which is always telling the way to a place, but never goes there."*

MRS GAMP HAS HER EYE ON THE FUTURE (*left*). *"With a leer of mingled sweetness and slyness, with one eye on the future, one on the bride, and an arch expression in her face, partly spiritual, partly spirituous . . . Mrs Gamp rummaged in her pocket and took from it a printed card. 'Put that somewheres where you can keep it in your mind . . . I'm well known to many ladies, and it's my card. Gamp is my name, and Gamp my nater.'"*

SOUTHERN ITALY.

THE CARNIVAL.

FESTIVAL OF THE VINTAGE.

NAPLES AND VESUVIUS.

BENEVENTO.

GULF OF VENICE

PAPAL STATES

ADRIATIC SEA

MEDITERRANEAN SEA

AFRICA

SCALE
Miles.

Longitude East from Greenwich

reads it, a personal kindness", his circumstances were such that, in April, he had to ask his friend, Mitton, to lend him £100 until June.

Dickens realised clearly enough when he saw accounts for *A Christmas Carol* that he must reduce his expenses. But it was not easy to alter the style of living to which he was now accustomed. He now moved in fashionable society. He had the large Devonshire Terrace house. He kept servants and entertained. It seemed that his best course would be to let his house and take his family to Italy for a year. The cost of living in Italy was far lower than in England and, besides this, there would be fewer demands on his time. He would be free to write another Christmas book which might redress the disappointment of the first.

On 2 July 1844, two days after the last number of *Martin Chuzzlewit* had been published, the Dickens family set off for Italy. A large travelling-carriage had been bought from the Pantechnicon near Belgrave Square. "I had two large Imperials on the roof," he recorded later in *The Uncommercial Traveller*, "other fitted storage for luggage in front, and other up behind; I had a net for books overhead, great pockets in all the windows, a leathern pouch or two hung up for odds and ends, and a reading-lamp fixed in the back of the chariot in case I should be benighted." One of Dickens's descendants, Mrs Stuart Dickens McHugh, was to add another detail about the travelling arrangements, evidently from informa-

tion handed down: "The only difficulty of the journey was the timing of urgent needs to stop in secluded places by the wayside for the purpose, otherwise fulfilled by the travelling chamber-pots in woven and lidded baskets."

Their journey was a complicated one. From Dover they sailed to Boulogne and thence by road to Paris. After two days at the Hôtel Meurice they continued by road to Châlons – the ninety-six bells on the four horses jingling all the way. They were then loaded aboard a steamboat and chugged down the Rhône to Lyons. From Lyons they

THE PALAZZO PESCHIERE, GENOA. *"There is no palace (in Naples) like the Peschiere for architecture, situation, gardens, or rooms. It is a great triumph to me, too, to find how cheap it is."*

NINETEENTH CENTURY MAP OF SOUTHERN ITALY *by John Tallis, far left.*

ST PETER'S, ROME, *looked immense in the distance. "The beauty of the Piazza, on which it stands, nothing can exaggerate."*

PORTRAIT OF DICKENS *by Charles Martin, 1843. When this picture was published, the accompanying text described Dickens as "small, but well-made; his look intelligent, and his eyes peculiarly expressive".*

VIEW OF GENOA. *"Terrace rising above terrace, garden above garden, palace above palace."*

rode in the travelling chariot once again, making for Marseilles, where they took ship for Genoa. Although new methods of transport were coming in, and steam had taken over on the rivers, it had yet to supersede the horse on French roads.

It was a time of transition in politics too.

In France, the citizen-king Louis Philippe (who in 1845 presented Macready with a "jewelled" dagger which proved to be a worthless sham) was becoming more and more unpopular. ("A shabby dog," Macready called him.) Louis Blanc was preaching socialism and "The Right to Work". Karl Marx had taken refuge in Paris before fleeing to Brussels. Events were moving inexorably towards the revolution of 1848.

Italy too was in an unsettled state. The Napoleonic Wars had given Italians a foretaste of being citizens of a united country — even though Napoleon and his brother-in-law Murat had never united all the Italian states. The Congress of Vienna had put things back to what they had been in the previous century and made Austria the dominant power. So, when Dickens landed in Genoa in 1844, Italy remained divided into numerous kingdoms and dukedoms with the Pope ruling a considerable territory from coast to coast across Central Italy, and the hand of Metternich, the Austrian chancellor, lying heavily on the entire peninsula. In 1846 there were to be great hopes for a change when a new pope, Pius IX, was elected. He introduced a number of reforms, but he refused to take up arms against catholic Austria when Lombardy and Piedmont rose against her in 1848, the year of upheavals. So any opportunity to unite the country was lost.

There is a comment in *Pictures from Italy* which shows how the division of the country among petty princelings prevented the spread of modern developments:

The then reigning Duke of Modena . . . claimed the proud distinction of being the only sovereign in Europe who had not recognised Louis Philippe as King of the French! He was not a wag, but quite in earnest. He was also much opposed to railroads; and if certain lines in contemplation by other potentates on either side of him had been executed, would have probably enjoyed the satisfaction of having an omnibus plying to and fro across his not very vast dominions, to forward travellers from one terminus to another.

Many of Dickens's descriptions emphasise the poverty and backwardness that he encountered. When the family was settled in the Villa Bagnerello in Albaro, the local people would come barefooted into the kitchen to sell fruit and vegetables to the cook. He was appalled by the fleas that infested everything – the dogs, the stables, and especially the people. He would see little family groups sitting by the roadside searching one another's heads for lice. "What a sad place Italy is!" he wrote to Count D'Orsay, "a country gone to sleep." But it was certainly a cheap country in which to live, with white wine at a penny farthing a pint.

Before coming to Italy, Dickens had started to learn the language. He attended two lessons a week in London, and in Genoa he continued his studies under a local teacher. It is surprising that he should confess to making only slow progress. His French, too, at this time, was not good enough for him to converse in it fluently, although he could read it fairly comfortably. But before very long Dickens became an excellent linguist and was at home in both languages. It has been suggested that people who are good at shorthand are often

equally good with languages. Dickens was certainly a good shorthand writer, which might explain his facility with French and Italian. It is interesting to note that, even while learning languages, he did not allow his skill with shorthand to lapse. Before sending the manuscript of *The Chimes* to England, he made a shorthand transcript which he retained in case the original was lost. This second little Christmas book had been thought out in some detail, but Dickens could find neither a suitable title nor a theme which would relate the episodes. He was getting exasperated, puzzling over these problems, when to his joy one October Sunday, all the bells of Genoa seemed to ring out the answer in unison. In a flash he had the title and the theme, and could begin to write. Off to London went the message: "We have heard THE CHIMES at midnight, Master Shallow!"

Dickens intended this new book to be "a great blow for the poor". It was a bitter attack on those contemporary economists and administrators who worked on the assumption that "the poor were born bad".

GRAND CANAL, VENICE. *"On we went, floating towards the heart of the strange place – clusters of houses, churches, heaps of stately buildings growing out of it."*

AT ALBARO. *"Everybody wears a dress. Mine extremely theatrical: Masaniello to the life . . . The moustaches are glorious!"*

A CHRISTMAS CAROL

Ebenezer Scrooge was a kind and open-hearted boy, but as the years have passed he has become a clutching grinding old curmudgeon who lives alone and denies himself every joy in life. He begrudges spending money on coals to warm his office clerk and naturally refuses to make any contributions to charity. One Christmas Eve in his gloomy lodgings, Scrooge is visited by the ghost of his former partner, Jacob Marley, who has been condemned to a life without rest or peace because of his devotion to money. Marley's ghost warns Scrooge that this will be his fate also unless he pays attention to the three spirits who will shortly appear.

The Spirit of Christmas Past arrives first and takes Scrooge back to his schooldays and then to the time when he was apprenticed to jovial Mr Fezziwig, whose simple generosity is held up as an example. Then the Spirit of Christmas Present takes Scrooge to the home of his clerk, Bob Cratchit, whose poor family manage to keep Christmas as it should be kept, even though their hearts are saddened that their crippled child, Tiny Tim, might soon be taken from them. Scrooge's pity is aroused. He is also stung when he hears Mrs Cratchit call him "an odious, stingy, unfeeling man". The Spirit also takes him to see how his nephew keeps Christmas, and Scrooge is dismayed to learn how people despise him.

Finally, the Spirit of Christmas Yet to Come shows Scrooge how the world reacts to his death. Old-clothes women strip the hangings from the bed while his corpse is still lying there; business colleagues dismiss the news with a shrug. Remorselessly the Spirit takes him from one harrowing scene to another before pointing to the gravestone bearing the name SCROOGE. The Spirit vanishes into the curtains of the room and Scrooge awakens to find everything has been a dream. He resolves to keep Christmas in the future. He buys the Cratchits the biggest turkey on the stall, sends a generous subscription to charity, raises Bob Cratchit's salary, and from thenceforth is a reformed character who keeps Christmas properly.

It assailed their proposition that a poor man had no right to marry until he could support a family, and similar notions which lay behind the new Poor Law. The book reflected much of the teaching of Thomas Carlyle, whose works were a great influence upon Dickens. Being convinced that Carlyle would welcome the book enthusiastically, Dickens proposed to return to London for a day or two at the end of 1844 in order to read the book aloud to Carlyle and one or two other close friends. So, accompanied by his servant, Louis Roche, he set out from Genoa on 6 November. After a hurried tour of Northern Italy, he crossed the Alps, reached Paris and journeyed on to London, meeting his friends in the Piazza Coffee House, Covent Garden, at almost the precise time he had promised. On 3 December, the reading was given at John Forster's house in Lincoln's Inn Fields. Daniel Maclise, who made a sketch of the occasion, reported how things had gone in a letter to Dickens's wife: "There was not a dry eye in the house . . . I do not think there ever was such a triumphant hour for Charles." (See page 65.) A second reading was given a day or two later and the triumph was repeated. But the visit was very brief. Soon Dickens was on his way back to Genoa, possibly musing on the idea of reading to larger audiences one day.

During his stay in Genoa, Dickens again

exercised the mesmeric powers he had already practised on his wife. It so happened that a Swiss banker, Emile de la Rue, and his English wife were also staying in Genoa at this time. Madame de la Rue was suffering from some form of mental or nervous disorder. It took distressing forms. There were times when she seemed perfectly all right. Then she would have spells when her body would become twisted and contorted. And there were dreadful times when she believed that she was haunted by a phantom. Her medical advisers seemed powerless to cure her and her husband became distracted with anxiety.

It occurred to Dickens that mesmerism might be helpful in dealing with a case such as this. He therefore suggested it to the husband, and in due course was asked to see what he could do at the next attack. So began an unhappy episode, the whole truth of which is not really known. It seems that Madame de la Rue had a number of severe attacks, some of them coming late at night. It also seems that Dickens's treatment proved effective and won the confidence of the lady's husband. When Dickens and his wife made a tour of Italy in the spring of 1845, the de la Rues accompanied them, staying at the same hotels. On a number of occasions, Emile de la Rue had to call Dickens from his bed to come and rescue Madame from the terrors which possessed her. But whereas Emile gladly acquiesced in the mesmeric treatment, Catherine Dickens did not. She was deeply suspicious of Charles's absence half the night in another woman's bedroom, and did not hide her resentment. She treated the de la Rues with cold hostility, which Dickens tried to excuse by saying she was unwell. Eventually, however, he was obliged to tell them the truth, which he found extremely painful to

SCROOGE WITH THE SPIRIT OF CHRISTMAS PRESENT. *In a snowy scene, from the 1938 MGM production, Scrooge, played by Reginald Owen, chats with the Spirit of Christmas Present. The film was memorable for its photographic effects.*

SCROOGE AND MARLEY'S
GHOST, *above and right.* " '*But
you were always a good man of
business, Jacob,' faltered Scrooge.
'Business!' cried the Ghost,
wringing its hands. 'Mankind
was my business. The common
welfare was my business; charity,
mercy, forbearance, and
benevolence were, all my
business.' " A scene from the
1938 film production by MGM.
Leo G. Carroll played the Ghost.
Lionel Barrymore was originally
to have played Scrooge, but, due
to poor health, the role was given
to Reginald Owen.*

THE GHOST OF CHRISTMAS
PRESENT *(right). "There sat a
jolly Giant, glorious to see, who
bore a glowing torch not unlike
Plenty's horn."*

JACOB MARLEY'S GHOST,
*opposite. "The same face: the very
same. Marley in his pig-tail . . .
The chain he drew was clasped
about his middle. It was long,
and wound about him like a tail:
and it was made of cash-boxes,
keys, padlocks, ledgers, deeds,
and heavy purses wrought in
steel."*

do. Probably this marked the beginning of that estrangement which finally led to the breakdown of the Dickens marriage.

While in Italy, Dickens had written a number of long descriptive letters to various friends. These were to form the basis for his next travel book, *Pictures from Italy*. In it, he gave an excellent account of how Italy appeared to an English traveller at that time. He did not recount, however, the accident which befell him during his residence at Albaro. Genoa was then a walled city, the gates of which were locked every night. When Dickens was invited there to dinner one evening, he suddenly realised that time was getting on and that, unless he departed immediately and ran as hard as he could, he would not get through the gates before they were closed. The night was pitch dark and he failed to see a pole placed across the road at waist-height until he had somersaulted over it. He lay in the dust badly shaken but was amazed to find that he had not broken any bones, although his clothes had suffered. He was not well, however, for some days afterwards, and it is probable that some permanent damage was done to his kidneys which affected him later in life.

The Dickens family left Italy in June 1845 and travelled home via Switzerland, Germany and Belgium. Back in England, Dickens devoted himself, heart and soul, to theatricals. He played Captain Bobadil in Ben Jonson's *Every Man in his Humour*, which was presented at the Royal Theatre,

Dean Street, in September. This was a great success. Dickens relished his part and for some time afterwards would sign his letters "Bobadil". He was now working on his third Christmas book, *The Cricket on the Hearth*. Two others were to follow – *The Battle of Life* in 1846, and *The Haunted Man* in 1848. Of these five Christmas books, only *A Christmas Carol* achieved lasting popularity, although *The Cricket on the Hearth* had the distinction of being the most dramatised of Dickens's works during his lifetime and in the years immediately following.

The name "The Cricket" had already been put forward as the title for a proposed weekly magazine which Dickens discussed with Forster soon after returning home from Italy. Nothing came of this proposal, but the name was incorporated in that of the next Christmas book, and the general idea of a magazine was borne in mind for a later occasion. But something much more demanding than a weekly magazine was offered to him – the editorship of a new daily paper. His publishers, Bradbury and Evans, were to be the printers. Paxton, who later built the Crystal Palace, was to provide the greater part of the finance. The paper would advance Liberal opinions and cam-

paign for reforms in taxation policy, factory legislation, sanitation and other things dear to Dickens's heart. So when it was agreed to pay him £2,000 a year instead of the £1,000 originally offered, he accepted the post.

His first concern was to enlist the services of as many able journalists as possible, and soon he had assembled an imposing team. These included W.H. Wills (later assistant editor on Dickens's *All the Year Round*), John Forster, Albany Fonblanque, Mark Lemon and Douglas Jerrold. Dickens was accused of nepotism, however, when it was learned that his father had been appointed Chief Reporter, that his uncle, John Henry Barrow, was going as Special Correspondent to India, and his father-in-law, George Hogarth, was to be music and drama critic.

There were some hiccoughs before *The Daily News* was launched. When a respected member of the Stock Exchange failed for about £100,000, a financial crisis spread panic throughout the City. The newspaper's backers hesitated. It was feared that advertising support would be lacking. Bradbury and Evans, who had just invested in expensive new printing machines, foresaw grievous losses. Dickens himself lost faith in the venture and sadly handed in his resignation. Fortunately, the scare quickly evaporated. Confidence was restored. Dickens was permitted to withdraw his resignation and once more took his seat in the little office on the third floor of the Daily News Building in Bouverie Street. Work began in making preparations to launch the first number.

This was an anxious time. The old-established newspapers looked unfavourably on the advent of a rival. Satirical cartoons appeared, ridiculing the newcomer. On the other side, Dickens was itching to pay off old scores. He had not forgotten the shabby treatment he had received from Sir John Easthope, chief proprietor of *The Morning Chronicle*, when he had resigned from that paper in 1837. He was now determined to show Easthope how a daily newspaper ought to be run.

The Daily News duly appeared on Wednesday, 21 January 1846. The printing was poor, however, and it was greeted with derision by its rivals.

Fortunately there was a better production the next night and the paper recovered from its teething troubles. But Dickens and the publishers were already getting at cross-purposes; Mr Bradbury in particular

CALEB, THE TOYMAKER, AT WORK, *by John Leech, from* The Cricket on the Hearth. *"There were Noah's Arks, in which the Birds and Beasts were an uncommonly tight fit. There were scores of melancholy little carts which . . . performed most doleful music. Many small fiddles, drums, and other instruments of torture; no end of cannon, shields, swords, spears, and guns . . . There were beasts of all sorts; horses, in particular, of every breed . . . Caleb and his daughter sat at work. The Blind Girl busy as a Dolls' dressmaker; and Caleb painting and glazing . . . a desirable family mansion."*

CORNHILL AND LOMBARD STREET. *George Beadnell, father of Maria, Dickens's first love, was manager of Smith's Bank in Lombard Street.*

annoyed the editor. He made difficulties over salaries, and levelled accusations against John Powell whom Dickens had engaged as sub-editor, alleging that he was quite unfit for the job. Dickens wrote angrily to Evans about Bradbury's behaviour: "I consider that his interposition between me and almost every act of mine ... was as disrespectful to me as injurious to the enterprise." He told the firm he was "utterly disgusted" and should act accordingly. At

As my song I troll out
for Christmas stout
The hearty the true
and the bold
A bumper I drain and
with might and main
Give three cheers
for Christmas old.

Charles Dickens

VERSE *of a Christmas Carol sung by Mr Wardel at Dingley Dell.*

the same time he wrote to Forster: "I have been revolving plans in my mind this morning for quitting the paper and going abroad again to write a new book in shilling numbers." Then, on 9 February, after a short respite at Rochester to celebrate his birthday, he resigned.

He continued, however, to contribute to the paper. The account of his Italian journeys appeared in its pages under the title *Travelling Letters*, to be published in book form later as *Pictures from Italy*. Dickens also wrote a series of letters to the editor on the subject of capital punishment. He also contributed two poems with contemporary relevance. One of these, *The Hymn of the Wiltshire Labourers* was occasioned by a report of a meeting of agricultural labourers angrily protesting about governmental moves for "Protection of the Agricultural Interest" which would be gravely prejudicial to the ordinary labourer. A young mother at this meeting had boldly stood up to declare: "They say we be protected. But if we be protected, we be starved." One stanza of Dickens's poem read:

> The God, who took a little child
> And set him in the midst,
> And promised him His mercy mild,
> As, by Thy Son, Thou didst:
> Look down upon our children dear,
> So gaunt, so cold, so spare,
> And let their images appear
> Where Lords and Gentry are!

In the letters on capital punishment, Dickens argued that public executions, instead of deterring crime, tended to encourage it. He wrote:

Out of 167 persons under sentence of death in England, questioned at different times in the course of years by an English clergyman in the performance of his duty, there were only three who had not been spectators of executions.

In a lengthy discussion he examined the reasons why people committed murders, and considered whether fear of the gallows ever prevented them. He concluded that it seldom did, and ended by asserting his belief that capital punishment "cannot be a part of the law laid down by the Divinity who walked the earth". Freed from newspaper encumbrances, he was now ready to begin his series of major novels.

Dombey and Son
David Copperfield
Bleak House
Hard Times
and
Little Dorrit

MIDDLE PERIOD

ickens's determination, after resigning from *The Daily News*, to go abroad again and begin writing another novel, was put into effect without any great delay.

After all the disappointments since his return from America – the poor sales of *Martin Chuzzlewit*, the poor profit from *A Christmas Carol* and his unsatisfactory labours on *The Daily News* – he felt that, if he got back to his old trade of writing a novel in monthly parts, his old position with the public might be restored.

So once more – on 30 May 1846 – the Dickens family set off on their travels. The courier, Roche, resumed his former job. Catherine's maid, Anne Brown, was also in the party, together with two nursemaids and a cook. Catherine had no desire to meet the de la Rues again so, instead of returning to Genoa, they headed for Switzerland. On 11 June they reached Lausanne, and four days later settled in the Villa Rosemont, a rented house on a hill between Lausanne and Ouchy.

Ideas about characters and situations had been in Dickens's head at least since March when he had written to Lady Blessington:

Vague thoughts of a new book are rife within me just now; and I go wandering about at night into the strangest places, according to my usual propensity at such a time – seeking rest and finding none.

At Lausanne he was able to settle down, especially when the box arrived from England containing his books and the little figures he liked to have on his desk while he wrote. Then, on 27 June 1846 (as he told

Forster), he "BEGAN DOMBEY". When unpacking his book, he took hold of a copy of *Tristram Shandy* and told his family, who were helping him: "Whatever passage my thumb rests on, I shall take as having reference to my work." Then he opened the book at random, and read: "What a work it is likely to turn out! Let us begin it!"

F.R. Leavis has called *Dombey and Son* Dickens's first major novel. This is a matter for debate. *Martin Chuzzlewit* was a very fine accomplishment, even if the American chapters spoiled its symmetry. It must surely be reckoned as a major novel. On the other hand, Dickens was in better control of his material in *Dombey*. From the first page he knew where he was going. There is greater psychological depth in the characters – although Edith Dombey and Carker are not entirely convincing. The use of imagery – the waves, the sea, timepieces ticking time away – add richness to the descriptions. It exceeds *Martin Chuzzlewit* in pathos but lags far behind it in humour.

Dombey and Son was not an easy book to write. When Dickens began it, he also had in mind a Christmas book for the end of that year. The competing claims of *The Battle of Life* and *Dombey and Son* were a severe trial. The novel progressed so slowly that Dickens felt he might have to abandon the Christmas book for that year. "I am fearful," he wrote, "of wearing myself out if I go on, and not being able to come back to the greater undertaking [i.e. *Dombey and Son*] with the necessary freshness and spirit." He longed for the inspiration he obtained by walking the streets of London.

THE YOUNG DAVID COPPERFIELD *(far left), from the 1969 production of the novel by 20th Century Fox. The film's all-star cast included Edith Evans, Laurence Olivier and Ralph Richardson.*

GEORGINA HOGARTH, *Catherine's younger sister, who joined the Dickens household when she was fifteen after Dickens and his wife returned from America in 1842. She acted as nursery governess, and taught the children to read and write. After Dickens and his wife separated, she stayed with Dickens, running his house at Gad's Hill. She was with him when he died on 9 June 1870.*

DOMBEY AND SON

This novel is a study in pride. Mr Dombey is a proud unbending man. When his wife dies giving birth to a son, Dombey's hopes and ambitions are so centred on this son that he completely ignores his first-born child, Florence, although she tries hard to win her father's regard. The baby son's health fails when his wet nurse is discharged, and he dies. Florence is anxious to comfort her grieving father, but he cruelly rebuffs her.

The incident which led to the nurse's dismissal also led to Florence meeting Walter Gay, a junior employee of Dombey and Son. Their friendship arouses the jealousy of James Carker, Dombey's chief clerk, who promptly arranges for Walter to be sent overseas. When no news is received about the ship carrying him, both Walter and the ship are presumed lost.

Mr Dombey decides to remarry and proposes to a young widow, Edith Granger, whose elderly mother, the Hon. Mrs Skewton, is determined to sell her daughter in the marriage market for the best possible price and so maintain them both. Edith has little choice but to follow her mother's dictates, but she treats her new husband with iceberg coolness. Florence, who had hoped to gain a new loving mother able to melt her father's heart and bring happiness to the home, discovers sadly there is no chance of this happening.

Carker has been plotting to undermine Dombey, and, realising how things stand, gains Edith's consent to elope with him. She is aware of his duplicity, and agrees merely to obtain her revenge on Dombey. She rejects Carker's advances, and as the pursuing Dombey arrives at the hotel, she escapes. Carker dashes back to England with Dombey on his heels. At a remote railway station, Carker is suddenly startled by Dombey's appearance. In surprise, he steps back onto the line and is killed by a train.

Florence has meanwhile sought refuge from her father's unkindness at the instrument-maker's shop. Here Captain Cuttle is in charge in the absence of Sol Gills, Walter Gay's uncle, who has gone in search of news of the boy. Walter returns home, having survived the shipwreck, and his uncle arrives soon after. Walter and Florence are married, and depart on a long voyage to China. While they are away, the firm of Dombey and Son fails. Dombey dismisses his servants, sells his furniture and becomes a recluse in one small apartment of the big house. When Florence returns, she and her father are reconciled, and she takes Dombey to live with her and Walter.

THE LITTLE WOODEN MIDSHIPMAN. *"Anywhere in the immediate vicinity (of the East India House) there might be seen . . . little timber midshipmen in obsolete naval uniforms, eternally employed outside the shop-doors of nautical instrument-makers in taking observations of hackney coaches."*

It seems as if they supplied something to my brain, which it cannot bear, when busy, to lose . . . A day in London sets me up again and starts me. But the toil and labour of writing, day after day, without that magic lantern is immense!

Fortunately, a short holiday in Geneva revived him. "A week of perfect idleness has brought me round again," he declared, and he returned to Rosemont able to finish the remainder of *The Battle of Life* and push on with *Dombey and Son*. In November, the family moved to Paris, where they re-mained during the winter, apart, that is, from Dickens himself, who made a short trip to London in December. He was in Paris, however, when he wrote the chapter describing the death of little Paul Dombey. Like the death of Little Nell, this left him heart-broken. In the Preface, he told his readers:

I began this book by the Lake of Geneva, and went on with it for some months in France, before pursuing it in England . . . My remembrance wanders for a whole winter night about the streets of Paris – as I restlessly

PAUL AND FLORENCE DOMBEY. *This stained glass panel is on display in a window of the Dickens House Museum, 48 Doughty Street, London.*

MRS MACSTINGER *and her family (below) discover the absent Captain Cuttle. "The benefit I've showered on that man, and he runs awa-a-ay!"*

did with a heavy heart, on the night when I had written the chapter in which my little friend and I parted company.

After the disappointing sales of *Martin Chuzzlewit*, Dickens was naturally on tenterhooks to learn how *Dombey and Son* would sell. He was regretting, too, having broken with Chapman and Hall so intemperately. Bradbury and Evans were printers rather than publishers; he had worries about their capabilities in advertising his work and carrying out the other functions of a publishing house. But he need not have worried. Bradbury and Evans did an excellent publicity job. They distributed bills all over the country advertising the book, and sent hundreds of cards to business firms soliciting advertisements for the monthly parts. The first number of *Dombey and Son* appeared on 1 October 1846 and sold out almost at once. Extra copies were hastily printed but even more were required. By mid-November, Part 1 has sold almost 32,000, some 10,000 more than *Martin Chuzzlewit*.

Dickens was having a break in Geneva when he received the publishers' news. He

was much more excited by these figures than he was by the effects of the revolution which had just taken place in this canton.

'You never would suppose from the look of this town that there had been anything revolutionary going on. Over the window of my old bedroom there is a great hole made by a cannon ball . . . and two of the bridges are under repair. But these are small tokens . . .'

As for *Dombey and Son*, he declared this was a "prodigious success". Subsequent monthly parts were as well received as Part 1; sales even rose and, by June 1847, reprints of the earlier numbers resulted in 40,000 copies of Part 1 being in print. It is interesting to compare these figures with the sales of *Vanity Fair*, which Bradbury and Evans were also publishing at this time. Thackeray never sold more than 5,000 of any monthly number of his novel, which explains his resigned but half-admiring remarks that there was "no writing against Dickens".

Dombey and Son not only restored Dickens's confidence but put an end to financial worries. Never again would he doubt his abilities or feel that his public was deserting him. Moreover, the sums he now received from Bradbury and Evans were, in Forster's words, "so much in excess of what had been expected from the new publishing arrangements that from this date all embarrassments connected with money were brought to a close". The novel thus marked the end of an era in Dickens's life and the beginning of a new one.

It also marked the end of an era in the social history of England, where two simultaneous revolutions were taking place. Both of these are graphically described in *Dombey and Son*. The first was the rapid expansion of London as developers began to obliterate the surrounding fields and woods and build thousands of cheap houses. Dickens commented on this in his description of John and Harriet Carker's cottage:

The neighbourhood . . . is neither of the town nor country. The former, like the giant in his travelling boots, has made a stride and passed it, and has set his brick-and-mortar heel a long way in advance; but the intermediate space between the giant's feet, as yet, is only blighted country, and not town; and here, among a few tall chimneys belching smoke all day and night, and among the brick-fields and the lanes where turf is cut, and where the fences tumble down, and where the dusty nettles grow, and where a scrap or

two of hedge may be seen, and where the bird-catcher still comes occasionally, though he swears every time to come no more – this ... home is to be found.

Dickens explained that this cottage stood "near to where the busy great north road of bygone days is silent and almost deserted, except by wayfarers who toil along on foot". Road transport, in fact, was almost at an end. The railways had arrived, and the great days of the stage-coach and stage-wagon were over. While some towns which had been coaching centres flourished as great railway junctions, other never properly survived the change. Such was the town that Dickens wrote about in one of *The Uncommercial Traveller* papers:

It had been a great stage-coaching town in the great stage-coaching times, and the ruthless railways had killed and buried it.

The railways were particularly ruthless in London when the great terminus stations were being constructed. London Bridge had been opened in 1836. This was followed by Euston in 1838, Paddington in 1841, Waterloo in 1844, and King's Cross in 1850. In *Dombey and Son* Dickens described the devastating effect of these developments on north London.

The first shock of a great earthquake had, just at that

period, rent the whole neighbourhood to its centre. Traces of its course were visible on every side. Houses were knocked down; streets broken through and stopped; deep pits and trenches dug in the ground; enormous heaps of earth and clay thrown up; buildings that were undermined and shaking, propped by great beams of wood. Here, a chaos of carts, overthrown and jumbled together ... there, confused treasures of iron ... fragments of unfinished walls and arches, and piles of scaffolding, and wildernesses of bricks, and giant forms of cranes, and tripods straddling above nothing ... In short, the yet unfinished and unopened railroad was in progress; and, from the very core of all this dire disorder, trailed smoothly away upon its mighty course of civilisation and improvement.

Dombey and Son dealt very largely with the contemporary world, illustrating not only the upheavals caused by these developments, but the impossibility of standing against progress. Old Solomon Gills, the ships' instrument maker, realised only too well that the world had changed, new types of nautical instruments had been invented and his antiquated business was no longer viable. The old man was forced to confess: "I'm behind the time altogether, a long way. It's no use my lagging on so far behind it."

The last part of *Dombey* was published in April 1848. Not until May in the following year did the first part of Dickens's next novel appear. This was *David Copperfield*, quite a different book and very largely a

CAPTAIN CUTTLE (*above and left*), *with a hook instead of a hand attached to his right wrist. "Love! Honour! And Obey! Overhaul your catechism. When found, turn the leaf down."*

DAVID COPPERFIELD

David is a posthumous child, born after his father's death. His mother is a thoughtless, inexperienced girl, and when the designing Murdstone flatters her, she readily consents to marry him. David is sent with his nurse, Peggotty, to stay with her brother Daniel while the wedding takes place. Daniel lives at Yarmouth in an old boat, and has adopted two orphaned relatives, Ham and Little Em'ly. Returning home, David finds it greatly changed. His mother is dominated by Murdstone who is aided and abetted by his sister, Miss Murdstone. They so bully David that he bites his stepfather and is sent to school in Kent. While he is there, his mother dies. David returns home where Murdstone arranges for him to work in the bottling warehouse of his firm, Murstone and Grinby, and to lodge with the Micawbers. Impecunious Mr Micawber survives a spell in a debtors' prison and then decides to leave London. David decides to leave also, but is robbed of his belongings and money and so has to walk to Dover to find his aunt, Betsey Trotwood. She adopts him and sends him to school in Canterbury where he lodges with Mr Wickfield and his daughter Agnes. David takes a dislike to Wickfield's articled clerk, the fawning Uriah Heep.

After leaving school, David is articled to Spenlow and Jorkins, proctors of Doctors' Commons. Meeting again his old schoolfellow, James Steerforth, David goes with him to Yarmouth where Steerforth is attracted to the pretty Little Em'ly, and impresses the simple fisherfolk with his false charm. Though Agnes has seen through Steerforth, hero-worshipping David takes no heed of her warnings. It is not until David returns to Yarmouth to attend the funeral of Peggotty's husband and when Steerforth elopes with Little Em'ly, that David realises Steerforth's true character. Yet David never quite ceases to love Steerforth.

A little later, David meets Dora Spenlow and falls instantly in love with her. They marry and set up house, but David soon realises that Dora is hopelessly incompetent. When Mr Micawber becomes a clerk for Mr Wickfield, he discovers how Uriah Heep, now a partner in the firm, has been defrauding them and is planning to marry Agnes.

Steerforth has taken Little Em'ly abroad, but when he tires of her she comes back to London where Mr Peggotty and David find her. David has now become a successful novelist, but Dora's health has deteriorated until she can no longer walk. David is heartbroken when she dies, and his sorrow increases when Ham is drowned in a great storm off Yarmouth while trying to rescue a man who, when his body is washed up, is later identified as Steerforth.

At the story's conclusion Micawber denounces Heep and emigrates to Australia with the Peggotty family, while David and Agnes marry.

disguised autobiography. The earlier chapters looked back to the world of Dickens's early years, recalling not merely the London that he had known as a boy but the harsh experiences that he had undergone when he "began life on his own account". Murdstone and Grinby's premises were none other than Lamert's blacking warehouse where Dickens had laboured as a boy.

Modern improvements have altered the place; but it was the last house at the bottom of a narrow street, curving down hill to the river, with some stairs at the end, where people took boat. It was a crazy old house with a wharf of its own, abutting on the water when the tide was in, and on the mud when the tide was out, and literally overrun with rats. Its panelled rooms, discoloured with the dirt and smoke of a hundred years, I daresay; its decaying floors and staircase; the squeaking and scuffling of the old grey rats down in the cellars; and the dirt and rottenness of the place; are things, not of many years ago in my mind, but of the present instant.

The fact of his ever having worked in such a place had been kept a secret by all the family. When he left the blacking warehouse and went to school, the boys there had no inkling of his previous history. As he wrote in *David Copperfield* about the boys at Dr Strong's school and their ignorance of David's experiences:

What would they say, who made so light of money, if they could know how I had scraped my halfpence together for the purchase of my daily saveloy and beer, or my slices of pudding? How would it affect them, who were so innocent of London life and London streets, to discover how knowing I was (and was ashamed to be) in some of the meanest phases of both?

Dickens's intimate friend, John Forster, knew nothing of this history until early in 1847. It was then that the elder Charles Dilke mentioned to him that he recalled seeing young Dickens working in a warehouse in The Strand, or nearby, and had given him half-a-crown. Forster found this recollection hard to believe, and asked Dickens whether there could possibly be any truth in it. Dickens was silent for several minutes and Forster realised he had touched on a tender nerve. Although he did not pursue the matter, Dickens realised that he had better be frank about the incident and the period in which it had occurred. So he wrote a detailed account of these

THE MURDSTONES (*left*), *with David and his mother in a scene from the 1969 film version of the novel. The Murdstones, brother and sister, tyrannised David's weak mother by mistreating her unfortunate son.*

early experiences which Forster was later to publish in his *Life of Dickens*.

In the meantime, Dickens adapted this account, almost word for word, for Chapter 11 of *David Copperfield*. The account given to Forster concluded:

Until old Hungerford Market was pulled down, until old Hungerford Stairs were destroyed, and the very nature of the ground changed, I never had the courage to go back to the place where my servitude began. I never saw it. I could not endure to go near it. For many years, when I came near to Robert Warren's in the Strand, I crossed over to the opposite side of the way to avoid a certain smell of the cement they put upon the blacking-corks, which reminded me of what I was once. It was a very long time before I liked to go up Chandos Street. My old way home by the Borough made me cry, after my eldest child could speak.

When Forster received these autobiographical notes, *David Copperfield* had not been thought of. Dickens was still writing *Dombey and Son*, after which he wrote the

HUNGERFORD MARKET, *selling fish, meat, and greengrocery, stood on the site where Charing Cross Station stands today. In the hall were stalls selling pictures and prints. (From an engraving by T H Shepherd, c.1850.)*

DAVID COPPERFIELD AND THE
FRIENDLY WAITER. " 'He came
in here,' said the waiter, 'ordered
a glass of this ale – would order
it – I told him not – drank it, and
fell dead. It was too old for him.' I
was very much shocked . . . and
said I thought I had better have
some water. 'Why, you see,' said
the waiter, 'our people don't like
things being ordered and left. It
offends 'em. But I'll drink it, if
you like. I'm used to it.' "

Christmas book *The Haunted Man*. A revival of *Every Man in his Humour* was presented at Manchester and Liverpool. Then, in an enthusiastic effort to ensure the preservation of Shakespeare's birthplace at Stratford-on-Avon, he rehearsed his amateur company in *The Merry Wives of Windsor*, playing the part of Shallow himself. Eight performances were given in London during the spring of 1848. In addition to these activities he devoted considerable time and energy to assisting Miss Angela Burdett-Coutts in her social work.

Miss Coutts was the daughter of the politician, Sir Francis Burdett, and granddaughter of the banker, Thomas Coutts. On inheriting her grandfather's huge fortune, she adopted his name and used her money to finance a variety of charitable,

religious and philanthropic causes. She built the extravagant Columbia Market and blocks of neighbouring working-class tenements. She endowed several churches, and collaborated with Dickens in a scheme to rescue prostitutes from the streets, teach them skills in house-craft, and eventually arrange for their emigration to Australia.

In November 1847, Urania Cottage in Shepherd's Bush was formally opened. The organisation of this "home for homeless women" owed a great deal to Dickens. He interviewed candidates for employment on the staff; he drew up the rules and regulations for the home; he even selected the clothing to be worn by the inmates, rejecting a suggested drab uniform, and insisting on dresses of pleasant colours to bring some brightness into the wearers' lives. Yet he was by no means "starry-eyed" about the possibility of reforming these girls. Some, he believed, could never be reformed, and he was quite ruthless in getting rid of girls who were admitted to the house and then proved recalcitrant or unruly.

He had already dealt with the subject of prostitution in *Oliver Twist* and *Dombey and Son*. It was a problem which both fascinated and repelled the Victorians. Gladstone and R.M. Ballantyne prowled the midnight streets on missions of reclamation. The Pre-Raphaelites, in their search for soulful models, salved their ambivalent consciences by doing what they could to help some of the poor creatures whom they chose as suitable subjects for their paintings. Thomas Hood's poem *The Bridge of Sighs*, which dealt with the suicide of a prostitute by drowning, was one of his most popular works. How many prostitutes there were in London, no-one knew for certain. They swarmed about the West End and invaded the theatres. Their behaviour and that of their fashionable customers was a public scandal.

Dickens introduced two prostitutes in *David Copperfield*, and also gave a detailed description of a typical house of resort.

The house swarmed with inmates . . . It was a broad panelled staircase, with massive balustrades of some dark wood; cornices above the doors, ornamented with carved fruit and flowers . . . But all these tokens of past grandeur were miserably decayed and dirty . . . it was like the marriage of a reduced old noble to a plebian pauper.

Already Golden Square and surrounding Soho were in a reduced condition.

Although Dickens described this house objectively and realistically, some of the dialogue he put into the mouths of his fictional prostitutes was most unconvincing. Who could imagine a real-life Martha Endell standing on the muddy bank of the Thames and exclaiming:

"Oh, the river! I know that I belong to it. I know that it's the natural company of such as I am! It comes from country places, where there was once no harm in it – and it creeps through the dismal streets, defiled and miserable – and it goes away, like my life, to a great sea that is always troubled – and I feel that I must go with it."

Dickens nevertheless understood what real prostitutes were like. He had the opportunity to observe at close quarters a good number who came to Urania Cottage. He noted that many who were admitted would be very docile for a period of some months and show themselves keen to work diligently for their own reformation. But then they would be "seized by a violent fit of the most extraordinary passion, apparently quite motiveless, and insist on going away ... This is to my thinking, so distinctly a Disease ... that I would pay particular attention to it, and treat it with particular gentleness and anxiety."

In *David Copperfield*, both Little Em'ly and Martha are rescued from their life on the streets and, like a number of girls from Urania Cottage, set sail on an emigrant ship for Australia.

Dickens set great store on the possibilities for reformation offered by a new life in the developing colonies of the Antipodes. He sent two of his sons to Australia, probably because he could not foresee either of them making a success in Great Britain. He had a firm belief that even a Wilkins Micawber who had failed in whatever he had turned his hand to at home would undoubtedly

ALDGATE. *En route to Salem House, David arrived at The Blue Boar, near to the Bull Inn here, in Aldgate Avenue. (From a nineteenth century engraving by T H Shepherd.)*

MR WILKINS MICAWBER. *In London, David lodged with the Micawbers, and found the family plagued by creditors who called at all hours. "At these times, Mr Micawber would be transported with grief and mortification . . . but within half an hour afterwards, he would polish up his shoes . . . and go out, humming a tune, with a greater air of gentility than ever."*

become the Port Middlebay District Magistrate if he could get to Australia.

Emigration increased greatly during Dickens's lifetime. Until 1830, the numbers leaving this country never exceeded 30,000 a year. In that year they doubled and by 1832 had reached 100,000. By the end of the 1840s about a quarter of a million people were leaving these shores annually. Of course, not all these emigrants went to Australia. Many went to the United States, Canada and South Africa. Some 300,000 joined the California gold rush in 1849 (the Forty-Niners).

Conditions on emigrant ships were often very bad indeed. There is evidence that unscrupulous shipowners circumvented the efforts of the government to ensure proper victualling, sanitation and so on. There is a story of a ship's drinking-water casks being filled with water from the River Mersey just before the ship sailed. People who had emigrated and then wished to return home faced as difficult, or even worse, conditions. In *American Notes*, Dickens described such a group who were travelling in the same ship as he was, bound for Liverpool. While the after-cabin passengers (of whom Dickens was one) lived in luxury, these unfortunate people were enduring great hardships. One man had no sustenance throughout the entire voyage apart from the bones and scraps of fat he took from the plates removed from the cabin dining-table.

In *David Copperfield*, the ship taking the Micawbers, Peggottys, Little Em'ly and Martha off to their new life is described in romantic terms. David is the narrator.

I seemed to stand in a picture by Ostade. It was such a strange scene . . . Among the great beams, bulks, and ringbolts of the ship, and the emigrant berths, and chests, and bundles, and barrels, and heaps of miscellaneous baggage – talking, laughing, crying, eating and drinking.

As David watched the ship off Gravesend as it was about to sail:

It was then calm, radiant sunset. She lay between us and the red light: and every taper line and spar was visible against the glow. A sight at once so beautiful, so mournful, and so hopeful . . . I never saw.

David Copperfield touched on many other matters besides prostitution and emigration. In the episodes of David's courtship of Dora Spenlow, Dickens recounted his own love-affair with Maria Beadnell.

She was more than human to me. She was a Fairy, a Sylph. I don't know what she was – anything that no-one ever saw, and everything that everybody ever wanted. I was swallowed up in an abyss of love in an instant. There was no pausing on the brink; no looking down, or looking back; I was gone, headlong, before I had sense to say a word to her.

But Dora was not the tantalising flirt that Maria had been, and Dickens refrained from spoiling his idyllic fiction by recounting the bitter story of Maria's coldness and their eventual moving apart.

In this novel he also looked back at his father's financial problems, and drew a portrait of his father in Mr Micawber. Many of the latter's high-flown phrases originated with John Dickens:

Never do tomorrow what you can do today. Procrastination is the thief of time. Collar him!

and
Annual income twenty pounds, annual expenditure

nineteen nineteen six, result happiness. Annual income twenty pounds, annual expenditure twenty pounds ought and six, result misery. The blossom is blighted, the leaf is withered, the God of day goes down upon the dreary scene, and – in short, you are for ever floored.

David Copperfield appeared in monthly parts from May 1849 to November 1850. In March 1850, the first number of the weekly magazine that Dickens had hankered after for years eventually made its appearance. It was entitled *Household Words* and, from now until his death, Dickens was to take on the responsibility for a periodical. This was to involve hours of work, reading countless manuscripts, amending many of those he accepted, inviting fellow novelists to contribute serials and, later, devising themes for Christmas numbers which would accommodate stories from a number of different hands. He wrote many articles himself for his magazines; one of his lengthier contributions to *Household Words* was *A Child's History of England*, which appeared intermittently in 1851.

DAVID WITH AGNES WICKFIELD *in a scene from the 1969 Omnibus production. The film's star cast included Wendy Hiller, Ron Moody, Michael Redgrave, Laurence Olivier, Ralph Richardson and Anna Massey, with Robin Phillips as David, and Susan Hampshire as Agnes Wickfield above.*

POSTER FOR THE FILM *produced by MGM, and starring W C Fields, Basil Rathbone and Maureen O'Sulliven in the key roles.*

STEERFORTH'S BODY *is washed up on the beach. A scene from the 1969 film version of the novel.*

BLEAK HOUSE

Before her marriage, Lady Dedlock, wife of Sir Leicester Dedlock, Baronet, secretly bore a child to her lover, Captain Hawdon. The child, Ester Summerson, has been brought up ignorant of her parentage, but she has been educated by her guardian, John Jarndyce, who takes her to be housekeeper at his home, Bleak House. He also has guardianship of two wards of court: Ada Clare and Richard Carstone. These two fall in love, but Richard cannot settle to any profession. He hopes to receive a big legacy when the case of Jarndyce versus Jarndyce is settled, though his guardian has no such confidence.

The lawyer Tulkinghorn hates the haughty Lady Dedlock. When she betrays unwonted emotion on recognising the handwriting on some legal documents, Tulkinghorn suspects something and begins to make enquiries. He discovers the writer of the papers was a man called Nemo who committed suicide in wretched circumstances.

Guppy, a lawyer's clerk, is in love with Esther, and proposes to her, but she refuses him. Meanwhile, Lady Dedlock's portrait reminds Guppy of someone he knows but cannot place.

Tulkinghorn's enquiries lead him to Jo the crossing-sweeper, who had taken a veiled lady to Nemo's grave and now recognises the dress she had worn. Guppy discovers that Nemo was Captain Hawdon, and that he and Lady Dedlock were Esther's parents. Jo contracts a smallpox and passes it to Esther, who is left badly disfigured. She puts all thoughts of marriage out of her head, although she had been attracted to the doctor, Allan Woodcourt. When Guppy sees her, he promptly rescinds any declaration she might think he had made.

Tulkinghorn eventually obtains a sample of Hawdon's writing, proving that he was Nemo. He confronts Lady Dedlock and threatens to expose her. Later, he is found shot dead in his chambers. Detective Bucket arrests an innocent man before he finds the true culprit: Lady Dedlock's maid, Hortense. Bucket uncovers Lady Dedlock's secret and he informs her shocked husband, who has a paralytic stroke. Lady Dedlock herself has fled. Bucket and Esther set out to find her, but too late. She lies dead at the place where her lover is buried.

Ada confesses to Esther that she and Richard have been secretly married, but Richard is now gravely ill. Before he dies, the case of Jarndyce versus Jarndyce comes to an end because all the money in dispute has been spent on legal fees. Richard is now reconciled with Mr Jarndyce, whom he had blamed for all his misfortunes, and dies at peace. Finally, Esther marries Allan Woodcourt.

In November 1851, Dickens began *Bleak House*, its first monthly part appearing in March 1852. He was now at the height of his powers, and this was one of his greatest novels. It centred about the Court of Chancery, which Dickens pictured in his brilliant opening chapter as standing at the very heart of the fog which blinded and bewildered all the institutions of England.

Never can there come fog too thick, never can there come mud and mire too deep, to assort with the groping and floundering condition which this High Court of Chancery, most pestilent of hoary sinners, holds, this day, in the sight of heaven and earth.

Everything and everybody in the novel is somehow connected with the case of Jarndyce and Jarndyce – a case which has been in progress for years, becoming more and more involved, until eventually it comes to a premature close when all the legacy in dispute has been used up in legal expenses. As the lawyer, Mr Kenge, explains:

"The numerous difficulties, contingencies, masterly fictions, and forms of procedures in this great cause [on which] there has been expended study, ability, eloquence, knowledge, intellect . . . must be paid for in money . . ."

As Dickens was at pains to point out, such prolonged and ruinous cases were by no means fictitious. He wrote in the Preface:

At the present moment (1853) there is a suit before the Court which was commenced nearly twenty years ago; in which costs have been incurred to the amount of £70,000.

The novel was not an attack on Chancery alone. Dickens saw the legal fog spreading everywhere and on all sides preventing the reform of abuses. He had been concerned for years about the dreadful housing conditions in London. In *Oliver Twist* he had described the horrific slums of Jacob's Island, accusing Chancery of being responsible for their state. "Thirty or forty years ago," he had written in that novel, "before losses and chancery suits came upon it, it was a thriving place; but now it is a desolate island indeed." Now in *Bleak House* he resumed his campaign, realising from the reports of such men as Dr Southwood Smith that the prevalence of fever, which was threatening the lives of everyone, was due in the main to the insanitary conditions under which the poor were obliged to live.

England had suffered its first cholera epidemic in 1831. In two years it killed some 60,000 people. Then there was a respite until October 1848, when there was a second outbreak. After another respite, there was a third outbreak in 1853. South-

JO THE CROSSING-SWEEPER, *by Kyd. " 'Never done nothink to get myself into no trouble, 'cept in not moving on,' says Jo. 'But I'm a-moving on now, I'm a-moving on to the berryin ground – that's the move as I'm up to.' "*

THE DOCTOR FOR THE POOR, by J Leonard (1827–1897). Dickens's friend, Southwood Smith, daily attended the Sanatorium in Marylebone, the Fever Hospital, the Eastern Dispensary, and the Jews' Hospital. England's cholera epidemic of 1831 killed 60,000 people. In Bleak House *Dickens makes dramatic use of the dreadful 'fever' which claimed victims from all classes of society.*

wood Smith was one of the doctors appointed to inquire into the causes of these epidemics.

All this suffering might have been averted, [he reported]. These poor people are victims that are sacrificed. The effect is the same as if twenty or thirty thousand . . . were annually taken from their homes and put to death.

His report makes unpleasant reading. In North Street, where Irish immigrants were numerous and Irish customs – pig-keeping, in particular – flourished unabated, he found pigs roaming in and out of the houses, leaving filth everywhere. The stench in the whole area was dreadful. The privies in North Street drained into a ditch encircling a large piece of waste land which was continually under water. It was used as a huge rubbish dump onto which the collected ordure from the ditch used to spill out in wet weather. "Nothing," wrote Dr Smith, "can be conceived more disgusting."

Jo, the crossing-sweeper, lives in such a slum, called Tom-all-Alone's.

It is a black, dilapidated street, avoided by all decent people. These tumbling tenements contain, by night, a swarm of misery. As, on the ruined human wretch, vermin parasites appear, so these ruined shelters have bred a crowd of foul existence that crawls in and

out of gaps in walls and boards . . . fetching and carrying fever . . . This desirable property is in Chancery, of course.

Dickens had a great interest in education, shown in almost all his novels. In *Bleak House* he imagined what it was like to be illiterate like Jo the crossing-sweeper, who gets on in the "unintelligible mess" as he can.

Jo sorely hurts the innocent Esther Summerson by contracting fever in Tom-all-Alone's and passing the infection to her. Dickens thus showed the inter-dependence of rich and poor. The slums were everyone's concern. The fevers bred in them could not be confined there.

Bleak House did not touch on emigration but Dickens introduced as one of the main characters, Mrs Jellyby, whom he based on Mrs Caroline Chisholm, one of the leading proponents and organisers of emigration. Dickens had been very grateful for Mrs Chisholm's help in getting passages for the girls at Urania Cottage. When he visited her home, however, he was disgusted at its disorder and confusion. Although Dickens was a fastidious and meticulous man, his imagination thrived on disorder. He obviously enjoyed describing Esther Summerson's call at the Jellybys:

we found that lady in the midst of a voluminous correspondence, opening, reading, and sorting . . ., with a great accumulation of torn covers on the floor.

Mrs Jellyby's energies were entirely devoted to the Borrioboola-Gha scheme for sending some hundred and seventy families to the left bank of the Niger.

In ridiculing Mrs Jellyby and the Borrioboola-Gha scheme, Dickens was attacking those responsible for the ill-fated Niger Expedition. Already in 1848 he had published a scathing article on this expedition, which had been sent out by a group of well-meaning religious bodies. The idea was to form a settlement on the Niger. The leaders would enter into negotiations with the local native chiefs who were responsible for the slave trade still being carried on. They would ensure that the trade was abolished and establish a model farm to be run by free labour. Unfortunately, the well-meaning organisers had taken no account of the climate in that part of the world, nor of the prevalence of malaria and other tropical diseases. They entered agreements with the native kings, relying entirely on their good faith, with no suspicion of the duplicity habitual to them. Not surprisingly, the expedition met with a series of disasters. Three naval vessels had accompanied them, but one after another they had to withdraw as disease struck. The *Wilberforce* left first, and then the *Soudan*, "on whose small and crowded decks, death has been, and is still, busy". The *Albert* went last of all, navigated by its two doctors because the captain, officers and engineers were all disabled. It was a sad story of incompetence and stupidity.

While Dickens was quite entitled to attack the organisers of this particular expedition, he was hardly justified in his continuous criticisms of missionary bodies generally. Many of them did excellent work under great difficulties. Undoubtedly and inevitably they made mistakes but they gained experience which was invaluable in the subsequent development of the countries in which they worked. To Dickens, though, all overseas missionary activity was anathema. Thus, in describing how Jo the crossing-sweeper began his day he showed him sitting down to breakfast on the doorstep of the Society for the Propagation of the Gos-

THE FRIENDLY BEHAVIOUR OF MR BUCKET, *by Phiz. Police Inspector Bucket calls on the Bagnets pretending to be looking for a second-hand cello. He makes friends with the Bagnet children, "drinks to Mrs Bagnet with a warmth approaching to rapture" and hides his real purpose. But when Trooper George leaves, he follows him out, and steers him into a public-house, where he confronts him. "You must consider yourself in custody, George."*

MR TURVEYDROP'S DANCING ACADEMY, *from* Bleak House. *"It was a bare, resounding room, smelling of stables; with cane forms along the walls . . . Several young lady pupils, ranging from thirteen or fourteen years of age to two or three and twenty, were assembled . . . I curtseyed to a little blue-eyed fair man of youthful appearance. He had a little fiddle, which we used to call at school a kit, under his left arm, and its little bow in the same hand."*

pel in Foreign Parts. Then came the ironic comment:

He has no idea, poor wretch, of the spiritual destitution of a coral reef in the Pacific, or what it costs to look up the precious souls among the coconuts and bread-fruit.

At least, he was even-handed in his attacks on religious bodies. While ridiculing nonconformists such as Mr Chadband, he treated Puseyites such as Mrs Pardiggle with equal disdain.

Dickens had intended *Bleak House* to be set in a period some years prior to its date of publication but he could not help making it extremely topical. It was no accident that the hero was a doctor, because Dickens's friend, Dr Southwood Smith, was the leading exponent of many of the reforms Dickens advocated in the novel. He had drawn attention to the state of the over-crowded inner-city burial grounds and to the polluted water supplied to the denizens of London's poorer districts. And, as already noted, he had investigated the sources of fever and reported on the disgraceful living conditions he had come across.

Another of Dickens's acquaintances who provided ideas for the book was Inspector Field of the Metropolitan Detective Police. He was the original of Inspector Bucket, possibly the first detective of popular fiction – an interesting and ambivalent character, one of the many which make *Bleak House* such a remarkable novel.

A few months after its completion, Dickens took a step which was to make a great difference to his life. In December 1853 he agreed to give some public readings for charity. These took place at Birmingham Town Hall. He gave two readings of *A Christmas Carol* and one of *The Cricket on the Hearth*. Some 2,000 people came to hear him on each occasion and received him enthusiastically. Just as he had done to a small audience in Forster's drawing-room a year or two earlier, Dickens reduced these thousands to tears and laughter at will. Again he discovered what it was to have "power".

However, whatever ideas he might have had for following up these successes, he was unable to do so at this time. The affairs of his magazine *Household Words* urgently demanded his attention. The magazine's half-yearly profits had hitherto fluctuated from about £900 to £1,300. In September 1853 they had suddenly slumped to below £550. By March 1854 they were down to below £400. Something had to be done, and the ideal thing would be for Dickens to write a new serial for the publication. It was decided that this should not be a full-length novel; it would only be as long as five numbers of *Bleak House* and would run for five months. The snag was that Dickens would have to write weekly instalments, a requirement that he had already found very constricting when writing *The Old Curiosity Shop* and *Barnaby Rudge*. Nevertheless, whatever the difficulties, it was imperative to rescue *Household Words*.

A bitter dispute was then in progress between the employers and cotton-mill workers in Preston. As it dragged on month after month, it attracted the attention of the London newspapers. It also interested Dickens, who saw it as a subject for the novel he was beginning to conceive. There were, of course, other matters he wished to introduce – educational policy, materialism, theories about art and design, the laws on divorce, measures taken to ensure industrial safety.

Preparatory to beginning the story, Dickens read through a number of official publications such as the questions devised by the Educational Board for the examination of teachers. He also visited Preston to see the strike for himself. Although this was not a particularly rewarding journey, it must have provided some material. He had written home:

I am afraid I shall not be able to get much here.

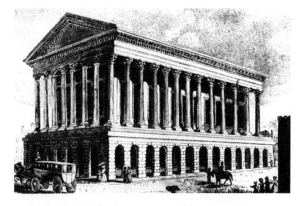

BIRMINGHAM TOWN HALL. *Dickens's first public reading was given here on 27th December 1853.* A Christmas Carol *took two hours with a ten-minute interval. 2,000 people attended.*

Except the crowds at the street-corners reading the placards pro and con; and the cold absence of smoke from the mill-chimneys, there is very little in the street to make the town remarkable . . . It is a nasty place (I thought it was a model town) . . .

The visit did, however, enable him to write an article for his magazine in which he set out his views on industrial relations with great clarity. He had found himself in a carriage with a "very acute, very determined, very emphatic personage, with a stout railway rug so drawn up over his chest that he looked as if he were sitting up in bed with his great-coat, hat, and gloves on". (Passengers in unheated trains would take care to have their travelling-rugs with them on winter journeys.) This emphatic personage had shown in the course of conversation with Dickens that he had no sympathy whatever with the strikers. "They want to be ground," was his opinion. He could see

DICKENS AS BOBADIL in *every man in his humour. Dickens was made up for the part by a dresser from one of the leading London theatres who gave him a peaked beard and black moustache, each hair being stuck on individually. After the downfall of Bobadil, the moustache was made to droop and the beard was dishevelled. Dickens wore real armour and "most enormous boots and spurs".*

HARD TIMES

The northern England borough of Coketown is a grimy industrial place where Josiah Bounderby's mill dominates the scene and provides most of the town's employment. The town's leading citizen, later to be its Member of Parliament, is Thomas Gradgrind, an exponent of Utilitarianism. He has founded a school where children are taught that only "Facts" matter, and any hint of "Fancy" is sternly suppressed. His children, Louisa and Tom, have been brought up under this system, and the novel is largely concerned with showing how it has warped their characters. Their fellow pupil, Bitzer, is led to reject all notions of generosity and compassion, and to put self-interest first. In contrast, Sissy Jupe, a pupil who has been raised in the circus, where "Fancy" reigns, remains unaffected by the school's teaching.

The lives of the Gradgrind children are dull and uninspired. On leaving school, Tom goes to work in Bounderby's bank, and Louisa enters a miserable marriage to Bounderby. Tom, being quite unprincipled, robs the bank and arranges for the blame to fall on Stephen Blackpool, a weaver in Bounderby's mill. Unhappy in her marriage, Louisa is tempted by a sophisticated politician, Harthouse, who seeks to seduce her. She nearly gives way, but at the last moment flees to her father's house.

Stephen Blackpool, even before being accused of theft, is facing many difficulties. His wife is a hopeless drunkard, but he cannot divorce her to marry the loving woman who would make him a good companion. He is also ostracised by his workmates for refusing to join their trade union. Leaving the town, Blackpool has the misfortune to fall into an unfenced mine-shaft where he lies injured and undiscovered for several days until he is finally rescued. He learns that his name has been cleared, but shortly afterwards he dies.

Tom Gradgrind, shown to be guilty, takes refuge in Sleary's Circus where he is pursued by his father and Bitzer. The latter follows the school's teaching of self-interest by offering to withhold from the police the proof of Tom's guilt – for a price. Sleary outwits him, with the assistance of the circus's trained animals, and Tom escapes. Gradgrind has had an object lesson from both of his children on the shortcomings of a Utilitarian education.

A RAGGED SCHOOL. *Designed for the raggedest children, ragged schools were ill-equipped, inadequately funded, and housed in the cheapest accommodation.*

nothing wrong with the action of the employers in locking the hands out, but everything wrong with the hands for combining to pursue their own struggle. Giving his own views on the situation, Dickens declined to use the terms Capital and Labour, preferring employers and employed. "I believe," he said, "that into the relations between employers and employed, as into all the relations of this life, there must enter something of feeling and sentiment; something of mutual explanation, forbearance and consideration; something which is . . . not exactly stateable in figures; otherwise those relations are wrong and rotten at the core and will never bear sound fruit."

He had already decided to introduce a circus troupe into the story to personify the Fancy that he wished to contrast with the Fact of materialists such as Gradgrind and Bounderby. So he asked Mark Lemon, editor of *Punch*, to let him have "any slang terms among the tumblers and circus-people that you can call to mind. I have noted down some – I want them for my new story." He also made a list of tentative titles for the work, including *According to Cocker, Our Hard-hearted Friend* and *A Matter of Calculation*, before he eventually decided upon *Hard Times*.

The serial began its run in April 1854. As he had expected, Dickens found the difficulties of getting the story into appropriate weekly instalments "crushing". But the effort was worth it. *Hard Times* is one of Dickens's best-constructed novels, although only recently have its merits been really appreciated. It did all it was expected to do for the sales of *Household Words*. Once it had been announced that "a new novel by Mr Dickens" would appear, sales shot up and the fears of the previous September were entirely dispelled. The new book opened with an attack on new teaching methods. That education should concentrate on imparting factual knowledge and deliberately try to repress the imaginative faculties offended Dickens's deepest instincts. He at once went into the attack:

CHRIST'S HOSPITAL *forms a striking contrast to the ragged school. There was excellent accommodation, although separate classrooms were yet to come. Here Coleridge and Lamb were educated.*

"Teach these boys and girls nothing but facts," ordered the government inspector. "Facts alone are wanted in life. Plant nothing else, and root out everything else."

The teacher, Mr M'Choakumchild, carried out these precepts:

He and some one hundred and forty other school-masters has been lately turned at the same time . . . like so many pianoforte legs.

Having thus attacked Utilitarianism in education, Dickens immediately turned to Utilitarianism in art. The Department of Practical Art had recently advanced theories in respect of the decoration of textiles, wallpapers and other articles, deploring the practice of depicting animals, flowers and fruit. This led to Sissy Jupe being rebuked in class for thinking it would be right to carpet a room with images of flowers:

"If you please, sir," said Sissy. "I am very fond of flowers."

"And is that why you would put tables and chairs upon them, and have people walking over them in heavy boots?"

"It wouldn't hurt them, sir. They wouldn't crush and wither, if you please, sir. They would be the pictures of what is very pretty and pleasant, and I would fancy —"

"Ay, ay, ay! But you mustn't fancy," cried the gentleman, quite elated by coming so happily to the point. "That's it! You are never to fancy."

In opposing Fact and Fancy, Thomas Gradgrind is the chief representative of the first. "Thomas Gradgrind, sir. A man of realities. A man of facts and calculation." He is supported by Josiah Bounderby, the mill-owner – "a rich man . . . A big loud man, with a stare and a metallic laugh. A man made out of coarse material . . .". In the opposite camp is the circus proprietor, the half-drunken, half-sober Sleary, with his lisped conviction that "People muth be amuthed, thquire!". Dickens probably absorbed a lot sub-consciously when he visited Preston. He wrote a brilliant description of the fictitious Coketown which encapsulated the features of all such mill-towns.

It was a town of red brick, or of brick that would have been red if the smoke and ashes had allowed it . . . It was a town of machinery and tall chimneys and vast piles of buildings . . . where the piston of the steam-engine worked monotonously up and down like the head of an elephant in a state of melancholy madness.

Among the workmen, Dickens concentrated attention on a handloom weaver, Stephen Blackpool, whose drunken wife was totally incapable of looking after herself, her husband, her home or anything:

barely able to preserve her sitting posture by steadying herself with one begrimed hand on the floor . . . A creature so foul to look at, in her tatters, stains, and splashes, but so much fouler than that in her moral infamy, that it was a shameful thing even to see her.

But Stephen had married her and was unable to divorce her. Had he been able to do so, he might have married Rachel, a young woman who loved him and was a constant support to him in his troubles.

The strike created fresh difficulties for Stephen when his refusal to join the union led to his being shunned as a black-leg. Through him, Dickens revealed his own sympathy with the workers and his contempt for the agitators who led them astray.

It was left to the dying Blackpool, regarded as a traitor by the workmen, to speak up on their behalf.

"Not rebels, nor yet rascals. Nowt o' the kind, ma'am, nowt o' the kind ... God forbid that I, that ha' known, and had'n experience o' these men aw my life – I that ha' etten and droonken wi' 'em, an' seet'n wi' 'em, an' toil'n wi' 'em, an' lov'n 'em, should fail fur to stan' by 'em wi' the truth."

At the climax of the book, when Stephen falls into an unfenced pit and is pulled out, only to die of his injuries, he makes a plea to the government for safety measures.

But he had little faith that working conditions, housing conditions and social injustices would ever be improved. "A muddle! Aw a muddle!" were almost his last words.

That England was "aw a muddle" was disastrously revealed when, in the autumn of 1854, Britain entered the Crimean War. Ever since he had reported parliamentary proceedings when he was a very young man, Dickens had a gloomy view of the abilities of the nation's rulers and administrators. But it took the news of the army's sufferings during the winter of 1854–55 to make him boil over with anger. Gross incompetence had let men die of cold and hunger when there were blankets and greatcoats and supplies of food readily available. Pettifogging officials had insisted on compliance with stupid rules and regulations when thousands of lives were at stake. In Dickens's eyes it was all an overwhelming example of "circumlocution", of "how not to do it". For the first time in his life he was driven to positive political action.

Austen Henry Layard, Member of Parliament, was an old friend of his. Some years ago they had climbed up Vesuvius together. At this juncture, Layard returned home having witnessed the Battle of Alma from the maintop of *H.M.S. Agamemnon*. Like Dickens, he was furious at the treatment of the British Army. He at once set about belabouring the government and, as he was a dogmatic, vociferous orator, he was (in the words of Justin McCarthy) "admirably fitted to be the spokesman of all those, and they were not a few, who saw that things had been going wrong, and were eager that something should be done".

Dickens was one of these. He met Layard at Miss Coutts's house and pledged his support. "Count upon my being Damascus steel to the core," he wrote. He defended Layard of the accusation of setting class against class. "No," he told Miss Coutts firmly, "it was the upper class who have put *their* class in opposition to the country – not the country which puts itself in opposition to them." He saw smouldering discontent

STEPHEN BLACKPOOL LIES DYING. *Having fallen into an unfenced pit, he is not rescued for several days. Mortally injured, he points to a star. "Rachel! In my pain an' trouble, lookin' up yonder – I ha' seen more clear!"*

FLORENCE NIGHTINGALE RECEIVES THE WOUNDED AT SCUTARI, *1856, by Jerry Barrett (1824–1908). Dickens was incensed by the incompetence which led to much needless suffering during the Crimean War.*

LITTLE DORRIT

Amy (Little) Dorrit is the youngest child of William Dorrit, a debtor who has been imprisoned for many years. Born inside the prison, Amy is "the Child of the Marshalsea" and he "the Father of the Marshalsea". Amy does needlework for Mrs Clennam, a stern, gloomy and wheelchair-bound religionist who lives in a dark old house where occasional strange noises presage the eventual collapse of the building. When her son, Arthur, returns from China after a long absence, he suspects that his parents have deeply wronged someone, but his mother refuses to comment on this.

Noticing her sympathetic treatment of Little Dorrit, Arthur wonders whether the wrong was committed against the Dorrit family, and begins to enquire into their history. He becomes acquainted with the family but, resigned to bachelorhood, he fails to observe that Little Dorrit has fallen in love with him.

Arthur enters into partnership with Daniel Doyce, an engineer and inventor, and resigns his share of his father's business. The engineering firm prospers, but its money is invested with Merdle, a fraudulent financier.

When William Dorrit finds that he is heir to a large unclaimed estate, he is able to quit the Marshalsea and take his family abroad, where he mixes in society and conceals his past. He too invests his money with Merdle. At a splendid banquet in Italy, William Dorrit has a stroke. He imagines he is back in prison and reveals his history by making a dramatic speech in the role of "Father of the Marshalsea". Inevitably, Merdle's overblown empire collapses, spreading ruin far and wide and bankrupting Arthur Clennam and his partner. Arthur finds himself in the Marshalsea where he falls seriously ill. Half delirious, he dreams that Little Dorrit has come to nurse him, which is in fact true.

Meanwhile, Blandois, a French criminal and reprieved wife-murderer, has discovered that Arthur is not Mrs Clennam's son. His real mother was not permitted by the family to marry his father, and he was brought up by Mrs Clennam in accordance with her strict principles to expiate the sins of his parents. Blandois has also discovered that Mrs Clennam has suppressed a codicil to a will under which Little Dorrit would have inherited a considerable sum. He blackmails Mrs Clennam with this knowledge. The shock to her is so great that for the first time in years she is able to leave her wheelchair and walk. She hurries to the Marshalsea to get help from Little Dorrit, but before she can return, the propped-up old house collapses and Blandois is killed beneath it.

At last Arthur recognises where his true love lies, and he and Little Dorrit are married quietly in the church next to the Marshalsea.

everywhere – "and it is extremely like the general mind of France before the breaking out of the first Revolution." The behaviour of aristocratic officers in the Crimea, the incompetence of aristocratic nominees in the civil service, and the stupidity of the aristocrats who packed the Cabinet, had clearly brought the country to the brink of disaster. "What a system!" he exploded, "where there are Chancery suits sixty years old, and admirals and generals on active service at eighty!"

Dickens was never so restless, despondent and angry as he was at this time. He could see that the country, like a ship which had never been cleaned of the barnacles on its hull, could make no headway. He could see that the barnacles on the nation's hull were the governing families and their dependants. These were not only incapable of properly administering the country but were determined at all costs to preserve their own position and privileges by preventing anyone else from doing so. The great study and object of these people who occupied all the seats of power was apparently to prevent anything being done. The conduct of the Russian war had made this crystal-clear. Soldiers had no tents while stocks were available only a few miles away. Horses died from lack of provender, when they could have been taken only a short distance from the lines where there was pasture for grazing. Men had to drop out from the line of march because the wearing of stiff uniforms with high stocks utterly exhausted them. These same uniforms, retained by the army authorities who loved the splendid show of scarlet on parade, made them conspicuous targets for enemy riflemen.

In the face of such incompetence an Administration Reform Association was formed in the summer of 1855 which both Dickens and Thackeray supported. Dickens was unable to attend its first meeting on 20 June because it coincided with the presentation of Wilkie Collins's play *The Lighthouse* which Dickens had produced and in which he was playing the lead. So he missed hearing Layard's violent denunciation of Palmerston. The government's own Blue Book, thundered Layard, revealed "records of inefficiency . . . ignorance . . . obstinacy," which were a shame to the nation. Palmer-

PORTRAIT OF JOHN SADLIER, MP. *Sadlier, MP for Sligo, was appointed a Junior Lord of the Treasury. When it was disclosed that he had fraudulently obtained £200,000 from the Tipperary Bank, he committed suicide on Hampstead Heath by drinking poison from a silver jug.*

ston replied in equally violent terms, condemning the Association and all its members, and having a special sneer at Dickens and his "private theatricals".

Dickens was invited to be the principal speaker at the second meeting of the Association when he made a bitterly witty speech in response to Palmerston's sneer.

The public theatricals which the noble° lord is so condescending as to manage are so intolerably bad, the machinery is so cumbrous, the parts so ill-distributed, the company so full of walking-gentlemen, the managers have such large families and are so bent upon putting those families into what is theatrically called "first business" – not because of their aptitude for it, but because they *are* their families – that we find ourselves obliged to organise an opposition.

The Administration Reform Association failed in its immediate purpose of achieving a speedy and thoroughgoing reorganisation of government. Eventually, however, and after stubborn resistance from the entrenched ruling class, its aims were fulfilled in a piecemeal fashion. In the meantime the attack on mismanagement had to continue, and Dickens resolved to do so in his next novel. In the angry, unsettled state that he was in, he found it very difficult to organise his ideas and embody them in the necessary

LITTLE DORRIT, *green cover. The title, spelled out in letters of uncompromising masonry and of heavy metal pieces chained together, is positioned around a prison gate to indicate the dominant theme of the novel – imprisonment. At the head of the illustration, a crippled Britannia is being led the wrong way by fools who refuse to be deflected from their purpose (a comment on the government's incompetent conduct of the Crimean War).*

fictional form. On 4th May 1855 he wrote to Leigh Hunt:

I am now ... in the wandering-unsettled-restless uncontrollable state of being about to begin a new book ... I sit down to work, do nothing, get up and walk a dozen miles, come back ... and go on turning upon the same wheel round and round and over and over again.

In the middle of that month, however, he did manage to begin *Little Dorrit* and it duly appeared in monthly parts from December 1855 to June 1857. He devised a plot of extreme complexity which served as a vehicle for biting criticisms of the Tite Barnacle family which dominated the government and, through the Circumlocution Office, affected all branches of administration. "The Barnacles were a very high family, and a very large family. They were dispersed all over the public offices, and held all sorts of public places." They ran the Circumlocution Office which "was beforehand ... in the art of perceiving – HOW NOT TO DO IT," (in other words, how to do nothing).

Yet for all Dickens's concern at this time about maladministration, this is not the principal concern of the novel, nor is the dominance of the upper class. *Little Dorrit* is about imprisonment and its various forms. At one level it is about actual imprisonment, and Dickens returned again to his personal recollections of his father's imprisonment for debt in the Marshalsea. The character, William Dorrit, is a second portrait of John Dickens, and a sadder portrait. Some of the high-flown diction of Micawber is repeated, but in a sadder mood. Dickens was at pains to show the effects of imprisonment on all members of the Dorrit family, and how the shadow of the Marshalsea remains on them even when they have come into a fortune and been released. Dickens shows how, in a sense, they remain imprisoned even when they travel abroad and the Marshalsea is far away. He then expands this notion to demonstrate that society as a whole is similarly imprisoned. Like the Dorrits, people in society "put a surface on" to hide the reality, to make the world believe they are something other than what they really are, and thereby imprison themselves behind the surface. In the novel, Mrs General is engaged by Mr Dorrit to impart gentility to his daughters, but Amy (Little Dorrit) cannot acquiesce, it being against her nature to dissemble in any way. Her father urges her in vain to "form a surface" and tells her:

"It is for your own sake that I wish you to have a – ha – truly refined mind, and [in the striking words of Mrs General] to be ignorant of everything that is not perfectly proper, placid, and pleasant."

One character who has managed to "put on a surface" is the financier, Mr Merdle, whose fraudulent dealings eventually lead to the collapse of his empire and the ruin of many trusting investors. Merdle therefore commits suicide by slashing his veins with a penknife as he lies in a bath at a public bath-house.

The room was still hot, and the marble of the bath still warm . . . The white marble at the bottom of the bath was veined with a dreadful red.

Dickens based this character on John Sadlier, M.P., who had engaged in fraud and forgery on a grand scale through his connection with the Tipperary Bank. When these crimes could no longer be concealed, Sadlier killed himself by drinking poison.

In *David Copperfield* Dickens had portrayed his youthful sweetheart, Maria Beadnell, as the delightful Dora Spenlow. In *Little Dorrit* he was to portray Maria again in rather different terms. It so happened that early in 1855 Maria, who was then married with a small daughter, wrote to Dickens reminding him of their former friendship.

LITTLE DORRIT. *Scenes from the 1987 Sands Films production, directed by Christine Edzard. Running from top to bottom: Little Dorrit, the Child of the Marshalsea (Sarrina Carruthers); Mrs Bangham, midwife in the Marshalsea Prison (Liz Smith); Mr Meagles (Roger Hammond), Arthur Clennam (Derek Jakobi) and Mr Doyce (Edward Burnham) in the engineering workshop in Bleeding Heart Yard; Lord Decimus Barnacle at the banquet (Robert Morley) with Flora Finching, Mr Casby's daughter, played by Miriam Margolyes. (Stills by Daniel Meadows.)*

He wrote a long letter in reply in which he told her:

As I was reading by my fire last night, a handful of notes was laid down on my table. I looked them over, and recognising the writing of no private friend, let them lie there and went back to my book. But I found my mind curiously disturbed, and wandering away

through so many years to such early times of my life, that I was quite perplexed to account for it . . . at last it came into my head that it must have been suggested by something in the look of one of those letters. So I turned them over again . . . Three or four and twenty years vanished like a dream . . .

He wrote to her again five days later after he had arrived in Paris. In this letter he made an amazingly frank confession of his youthful passion for her.

I have always believed since, and always shall to the last, that there never was such a faithful and devoted poor fellow as I was.

He went on to say:

It is a matter of perfect certainty to me that I began to fight my way out of poverty and obscurity with one perpetual idea of you.

So Dickens arranged to meet her again when he returned to London, but when they met, he was more than dismayed to find how greatly she had changed and that she was no longer the Maria he remembered. It is sad and unforgiveable that he should have introduced her into *Little Dorrit* as Flora.

Flora, always tall, had grown to be very broad too, and short of breath; . . . Flora, whom he had left a lily, had become a peony . . . Flora, who had seemed enchanting in all she said and thought, was diffuse and silly.

Little Dorrit contains much more than the Circumlocution Office, the Marshalsea, Mr Merdle and Flora. It is a wonderfully rich novel – rich in ideas, rich in characterisation, rich in incident, and written in a richly imaginative prose. It is in many ways a sad, gloomy book; because of this, it was not fully appreciated by most Victorian readers who were always hoping for another *Pickwick*. But today, many critics regard it as Dickens's masterpiece.

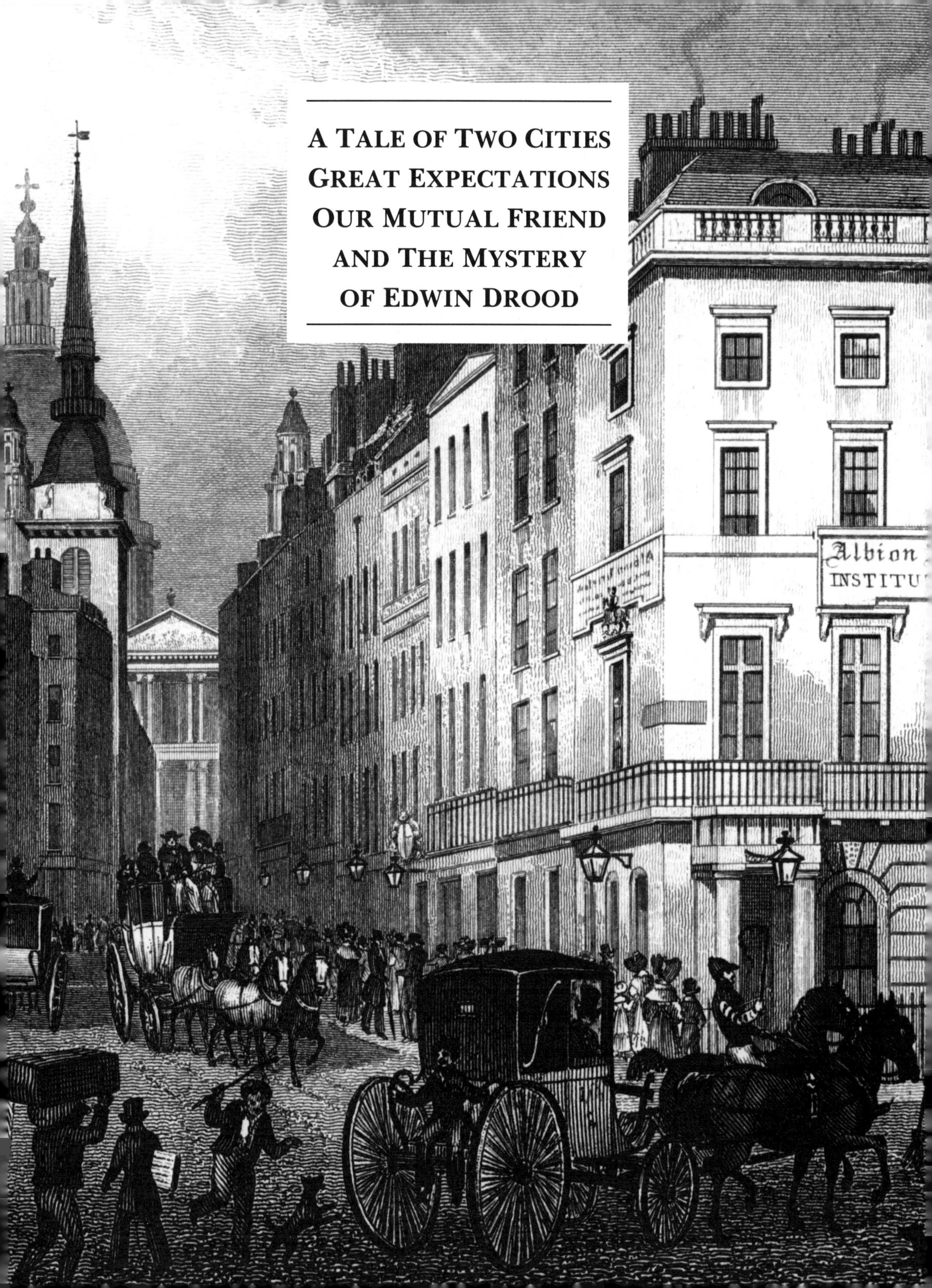

A TALE OF TWO CITIES
GREAT EXPECTATIONS
OUR MUTUAL FRIEND
AND THE MYSTERY
OF EDWIN DROOD

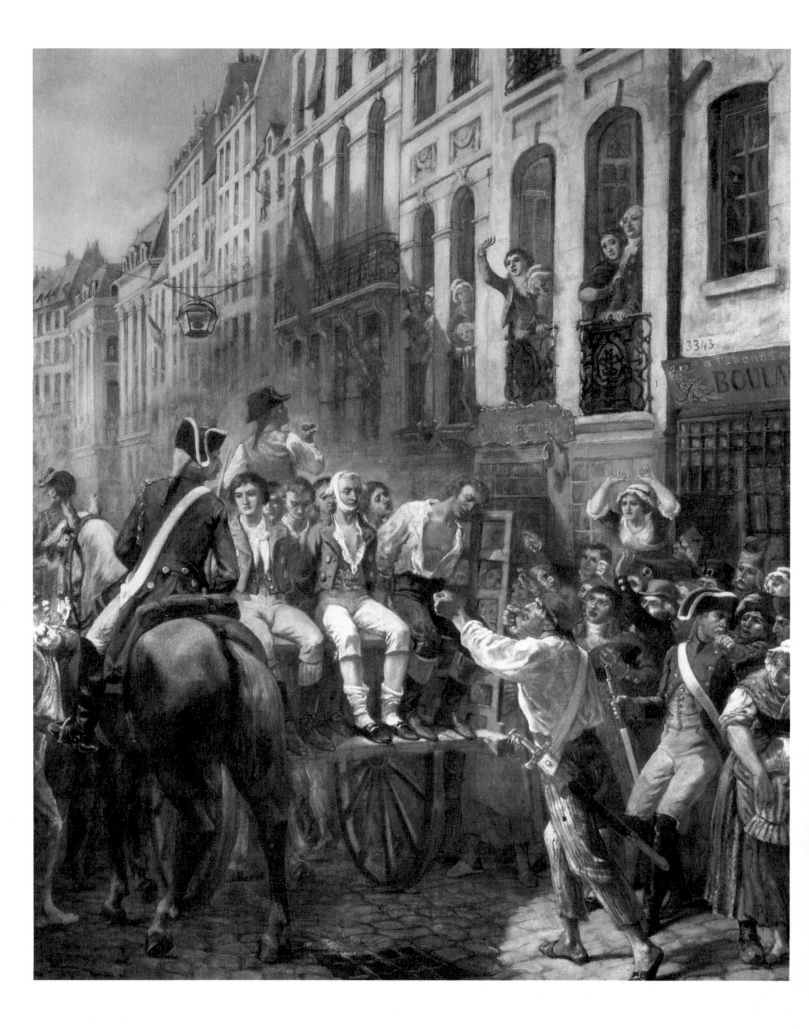

CHAPTER
5

FINAL PERIOD

The Crimean War and the agitation for administrative reform had greatly disturbed Dickens. Throughout 1855 he was deeply depressed. In January he wrote to Forster:

Am altogether in a dishevelled state of mind – motes of new books in the dirty air, miseries of older growth threatening to close upon me. Why is it . . . a sense comes always crushing on me now, when I fall into low spirits, as of one happiness I have missed in life, and one friend and companion I have never made?

The re-appearance of Maria Beadnell, and the subsequent disappointment when he met her, increased these miseries. When, on his birthday that year, he saw that Gad's Hill Place was up for sale, he might have felt that it offered a chance to return in some mysterious way to the time of his happier childhood; as a "very queer small boy" he had gone walking with his father past that very house and his father had prophesied that if he "were to be very persevering and were to work hard" he might some day come to live in it. Whatever hopes he might have had, he had few now of rescuing his marriage. Relations with his wife went from bad to worse and, as he confessed at this time, "The skeleton in my domestic closet is becoming a pretty big one".

Towards the end of 1856, when he was concluding *Little Dorrit*, Dickens began to rehearse another play by Wilkie Collins, *The Frozen Deep*, which was first produced the next January in the little theatre that Dickens had created in his London home, Tavistock House. This melodrama had been inspired by news of attempts being made to find the lost Polar explorer, Sir John Franklin. It concerned the rivalry of two young men for the hand of the same young woman. Both men find themselves on an expedition to the arctic regions, during which they are both placed in an extremely dangerous situation. One would undoubtedly have lost his life if the other had not made a valiant attempt to rescue him. In doing this, however, and saving a bitter rival, the rescuer sacrifices his own life.

Dickens was greatly affected by this drama. He would borrow the idea of two men in love with the same woman, one of them making a supreme sacrifice on behalf of the other, as the basis for his next novel. But

ROBESPIERRE AND SAINT-JUST LEAVE FOR THE GUILLOTINE *by Alfred Mouillard, c.1870 (far left). "All eyes are on Robespierre's Tumbril, where he, his jaw bound in dirty linen, with his half-dead Brother and half-dead Henriot, lie shattered . . . The Gendarmes point their swords at him, to show the people it is he." From Thomas Carlyle's* French Revolution, *Dickens borrowed some of these details; the horsemen abreast of Carton's tumbril, for instance, point him out in a similar way.*

DR MANETTE IN THE BASTILLE. *"A white-haired man sat on a low bench, stooping forward and very busy, making shoes."*

A Tale of Two Cities

Dr Manette, a French physician, has been imprisoned in the Bastille for eighteen years by order of the Marquis St. Evremonde. The Marquis had wished to prevent the doctor from disclosing what he had learned from attending a dying woman who had been raped by the Marquis. Dr. Manette, now a bewildered white-haired man engrossed in his work as a shoemaker, is eventually released into the care of Mr Lorry of Tellson's Bank in London.

When the Marquis's nephew, Charles Darnay, comes to England after renouncing his French citizenship, he is arrested as a spy. At the Old Bailey he is saved from the gallows by his defence lawyer, Sydney Carton, a clever but dissolute young man, who demonstrates his own close resemblance to the prisoner and therefore the unreliability of witnesses testifying to the identification of the prisoner. Carton and Darnay visit the doctor's house regularly and both fall in love with the doctor's daughter, Lucie. When she accepts Darnay's proposal, Carton solemnly promises her his utmost assistance should any person whom she loves ever be in danger.

In the Defarge's Paris wine shop, Defarge prepares for the day when the people will rise against their oppressors and his wife knits a coded record of those on whom vengance will fall. She is the sister of the woman whom Dr Manette attended. Madame Defarge and her husband know that during his imprisonment, the Doctor had written a paper describing his involvement with the St. Evremondes and vowing revenge. This paper was hidden in his cell.

On his uncle's murder, Charles becomes head of the family, and when the Revolution breaks out he remains in London. When one of his tenants pleads for him to come and give evidence on his behalf, Charles reluctantly goes to France and is at once arrested. Believing that Dr Manette, who had suffered so much under the old regime, could obtain Charles's release, the Doctor, Lucie and her baby, and their servant come to Paris with Mr Lorry. After a long wait, Charles is brought to trial and acquitted, but almost at once he is re-arrested. At his second trial, the paper by Dr Manette, in which he denounces the entire race of St. Evremondes, is read aloud. On this evidence Charles is sentenced to death.

On the eve of the execution Carton arranges for an English spy, who is a turnkey in the Conciergerie, to smuggle him into Darnay's cell. Carton half-drugs Darnay and exchanges clothes with him. When Darnay collapses, the spy carries him out and he is restored to his family. They leave Paris in the sorrowful belief that the unconscious man in their coach is Carton and that Darnay has gone to his death. On his way to the guillotine, Carton comforts a little seamstress under similar sentence who takes courage from him when she realises his sacrifice.

before this was to happen, he arranged to present the play again after its successful reception in London. It would be staged in the Manchester Free Trade Hall. This was a vast place, and it was clear that the amateur actresses of Dickens's company would never make themselves heard there. So Dickens took steps to replace them with professional actresses, and accordingly engaged Mrs Ternan and her daughters, Maria and Ellen. Maria took the part of the heroine. Dickens was loud in his praise of her acting – too loud, in fact – because he was most anxious to conceal that his thoughts were not so much with Maria as with the younger girl, Ellen, with whom, suddenly and completely, he had fallen in love.

This was the turning-point in Dickens's later life. He gave orders for a separate bedroom to be made for him at Tavistock House and soon the skeleton in his domestic closet could be hidden no longer. He and Catherine agreed to separate. Rumours went about that Dickens was having an affair either with his sister-in-law or with an actress. There were stormy scenes with his wife's relations. There were stormy scenes, too, with the publishers, Bradbury and Evans. Dickens had wished them to publish a "Personal Statement" from him in their periodical *Punch*. When they refused to do so, on the grounds that Dickens's private affairs had nothing to do with the readers of *Punch*, Dickens broke his connection with the firm and returned to his first publishers, Chapman and Hall. There were other repercussions. Bradbury and Evans published Dickens's magazine, *Household Words*. When Dickens founded a new weekly, *All The Year Round*, the older magazine was forced to close. His annoyance with Bradbury and Evans was not easily assuaged. When his eldest son married Evans's daughter, Dickens refused to attend the wedding.

It was most important that the new magazine got off to a good start, and this meant including a serial from Dickens's pen. Dickens set about developing the notion that he had borrowed from *The Frozen Deep*, combining this with ideas from Carlyle's book, *The French Revolution*, which Dickens boasted to have read several hundred times. It would also seem quite likely, although there is no proof of it, that Dickens had

UNDER THE PLANE TREE *in Dr Manette's garden – Lucie, Charles Darnay, Sydney Carton, Mr Lorry, and Dr Manette.*

SYDNEY CARTON WITH BARSAD THE SPY, *now a Gaoler in the Conciergerie (below). A scene from the 1958 screen version of the novel,* A Tale of Two Cities, *starring Dirk Bogard as the brilliant but dissolute young lawyer, Carton, seen here with Jerry Cruncher played by Alfie Bass. The film was produced by The Rank Organisation.*

1859. It is interesting to observe how each of these later novels contained the germ of the next. *Hard Times* had handed on the notion that things were "aw a muddle" to *Little Dorrit*. Now *A Tale of Two Cities* received from *Little Dorrit* the subject of imprisonment and especially the belief that the present is imprisoned in the past.

This was the second historical novel that Dickens had attempted. Like *Barnaby Rudge* it deals with upheaval, and like the earlier book it reflects Dickens's fears of possible unrest. During the spring of 1855, revolution had been often in his thoughts. He had feared it could engulf England itself:

> ... a bad harvest – the last strain too much of aristocratic insolence or incapacity – a defeat abroad – a mere chance at home [could turn] into such a devil of a conflagration as never had been beheld before.

read *Letters Written in the Summer of 1790 to a Friend in England* by a certain Helen Maria Williams. These letters related the story of a Baron du F– who caused his son, Monsieur du F–, to be imprisoned for a lengthy period. The resemblance of this Baron to Monseigneur le Marquis in Dickens's novel, and of Monsieur du F– to both Dr Manette and Charles Darnay, is so striking that it seems incredible that Dickens had not come across these letters. Certainly Dickens drew from a number of sources when preparing *A Tale of Two Cities*, and we know that Carlyle sent him two cartloads of books from the London Library.

The new novel began to run in the first number of *All the Year Round* on 30 April

By 1859 the immediate danger had receded, but things had not improved greatly. The reforms in the Civil Service advocated in the Northcote-Trevelyan report had never been implemented. Very little had been done in the realm of public health. Although many municipalities had indeed been spurred by the fear of cholera to improve public sanitation, pressure to do so was already declining. After the outbreak of 1853, it was believed that the danger was past. The government even dissolved the General Board of Health in 1858 and divided its duties between the Privy Council and the Home Office. Administrative lethargy was as evident as ever, and Dickens

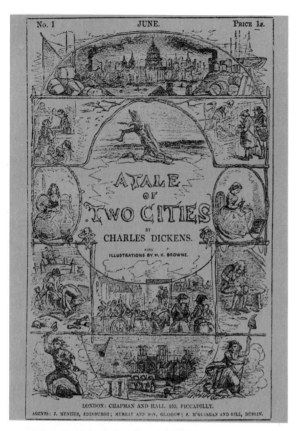

MONTHLY PARTS COVER (far left). While this novel appeared weekly in All The Year Round, monthly parts in green covers were also published. This was the last Dickens novel to be illustrated by Phiz. Several episodes are clearly discernible in the illustration – Carton defending Darnay, Tellson's Bank, Cruncher's grave-robbing activities, Dr Manette in prison, and the French Revolution.

MADAME DEFARGE KNITTING (left). " 'What do you make, madame?' 'Many things.' 'For instance –' 'For instance,' returned Madame Defarge, composedly, 'shrouds.' " In a scene from the 1958 film production, A Tale of Two Cities, the rebels conspire against their oppressors: left, Freda Jackson as the Vengance; centre, Rosalie Crutchley as Madame Defarge; and right, Eric Pohlmann as The Lawyer.

remained fearful of revolution as long as the present authorities remained in power.

He therefore used his novel to convey some of his own views about revolution generally. He had every sympathy with the underdogs but none at all with their excesses. He saw clearly how revolutions tend to get out of hand and revolutionaries become corrupted by power. He closed his novel by seeing "Long ranks of new oppressors who have risen on the destruction of the old".

From the time of its publication *A Tale of Two Cities* became one of the most popular of all Dickens's books. The first number of *All the Year Round* sold 120,000 copies, and later weekly sales remained around 100,000. Dickens had decided on two concurrent forms of publication. While it appeared in weekly magazine instalments, it also came out in monthly parts illustrated by Phiz (H.K. Browne). This was to be the last novel illustrated by this artist who had been closely associated with Dickens ever since *The Pickwick Papers*. The experiment with monthly parts was not sufficiently rewarding, however, to justify its being tried again when *Great Expectations* was serialised in *All the Year Round* a few years later.

Although many people hold that *A Tale of Two Cities* is their favourite Dickens novel, it is not a typical one at all. It has none of the elaborations of description and ramifications of plot which distinguish Dickens's twenty-part novels. It is largely devoid of humour and its characters, apart from Jerry Cruncher and Miss Pross, are not what we would regard as "Dickensian". Its plot was adapted, as already explained, from a romantic melodrama, and the novel is in consequence romantic and melodramatic. Inevitably, it was dramatised; as *The Only Way*, in which Sir John Martin-Harvey played Sydney Carton, it enjoyed one of the lengthiest runs in theatrical history, delighting audiences throughout the English-speaking world.

Though *A Tale of Two Cities* may not be the most typical of Dickens's novels, it does contain some wonderful passages which only Dickens could have written. The description in Chapter 2 of the Dover mailcoach ascending Shooter's Hill, its horses floundering through the mire as they labour to drag up the heavy vehicle, and the mist encircling them "as if they had made it all", is a marvellously graphic and memorable piece of writing. The descriptions of mob violence – the hanging of Foulon and the taking of the Bastille – are among the best things Dickens ever wrote. He followed Carlyle closely in his accounts of historical happenings, but a comparison of similar

POSTER FOR THE FILM of 1958, produced by the The Rank Organisation, and starring Dirk Bogarde in the leading role.

passages shows Dickens the superior in dramatic force. It is interesting, too, to compare Dickens's description of the storming of Newgate in *Barnaby Rudge* with his description of the attack on the Bastille, and note how the same imagery is used in both. It is employed sparsely in *Barnaby Rudge*, where the riot scenes are crammed with detail, but when Dickens needs a simile he finds it in the sea:

The rioters . . . rose like a great sea . . . and with such inconceivable fury, that those who had the direction of the troops knew not, at first, where to turn or what to do.

In *A Tale of Two Cities*, when Defarge calls for the assault on the Bastille:

With a roar that sounded as if all the breath in France had been shaped into the detested word, the living sea rose.

And when Defarge is swept over the drawbridge:

So resistless was the force of the ocean bearing him on, that even to draw his breath or turn his head was as impracticable as if he had been struggling in the surf at the South Sea.

In his later novels Dickens invariably took an idea and developed it in a number of quite different ways. He did this in *Little Dorrit* with the idea of imprisonment. In *A Tale of Two Cities* he took the idea of resurrection, or of being "recalled to life". The first section of the novel is actually entitled "Recalled to Life" and relates how Dr Manette is released from the Bastille after eighteen years and restored to his daughter and to his life as a doctor. Then John Barsad, the Old Bailey spy, is given a mock funeral so that he may disappear and be "recalled to life" in a new sphere of activity. Charles Darnay is recalled to life when he is acquitted on a capital charge, and he is recalled to life yet again at the end of the book when through the intervention of Carton he is smuggled out of the Conciergerie. Finally Sydney Carton is recalled from a life of idleness and dissipation to one of self-sacrifice in taking the place of Darnay and going to the guillotine.

Allied to this idea of the recall to life is that of resurrection. As he paces the Paris streets preparing his plans for the sacrifice that he is determined to make for the woman he has loved but lost, Carton recites the Biblical passage "I am the Resurrection and the Life . . .". Another aspect of "resurrection" was in the activities of so-called "Resurrection men" who not only robbed graveyards of newly buried bodies but, on occasions, committed murder to supply the needs of apprentice surgeons studying anatomy. Jerry Cruncher, messenger at Tellson's Bank by day, is a resurrection man by night, but he apparently confined himself to the opening of coffins. Not so Messrs Bishop and Williams who in 1831 offered the body of a fourteen-year-old boy to one of London's leading surgeons. Realising that the boy had been murdered, the surgeon notified the authorities. As a result the two men were caught and hanged. It was this crime, rather than the better-known one by Burke and Hare the previous year in Scotland, that ensured the passing of the Anatomy Act in 1832. After that date, bodies could be obtained for medical research by legal means.

It has been pointed out that the description of Lucie Manette could well be a description of Dickens's mistress, Ellen Ternan, whose photographs reveal many of the features which Dickens lists so meticulously (and unnecessarily) in *A Tale of Two Cities*:

. . . a short, slight, pretty figure, a quantity of golden hair, a pair of blue eyes . . . with an enquiring look, and a forehead with a singular capacity [remembering how young and smooth it was], of lifting and knitting itself into an expression that was not quite one of perplexity, or wonder, or alarm, or merely of a bright fixed attention, though it included all . . . four

Shortly after concluding this novel, Dickens began to publish a series of occasional essays in his magazine under the title *The Uncommercial Traveller*. These were largely autobiographical, describing visits to such places as the Chatham dockyard, the Liverpool dockside area, inns of court, workhouses, theatres and city churches. In some essays Dickens gave fascinating glimpses of his childhood, and in others invited readers to accompany him on walks around Gad's Hill and Cobham. While not everything in the essays is strictly factual, they afford an insight into his life and opinions. For instance, they show how concerned he was about the welfare of seamen exposed to the depravations of "land sharks", and of workers in lead-mills exposed to the hazards of handling dangerous substances. They also show how ready he always was to resume his old profession of investigative journalist. After the wreck of the *Royal Charter*, he hastened to Anglesey in order to see the place for himself and interview the clergyman who had taken charge of bodies as they came ashore.

In the summer of 1860 Dickens gave up his London home in Tavistock Square and made Gad's Hill Place his permanent residence. In another symbolic break with the past, on 3 September 1860 he burned all the accumulated correspondence of years.

PORTRAIT OF ELLEN TERNAN. *Precise information about Dickens's relations with Ellen Ternan is sparse. He met her when she was engaged to play the part of Lucy Crayford in* The Frozen Deep *at Manchester. He evidently fell in love with her, and in his will he left her £1,000 free of legacy duty.*

ON THE STEPS AT GAD'S HILL PLACE. *Standing, Katie, Mamie, and Charles Dickens. Seated, Henry Chorley, Charles Collins, Georgina Hogarth.*

GREAT EXPECTATIONS

The convict Magwitch escapes from the hulks while awaiting transportation to Australia. Wet and hungry, he comes across Pip in a lonely churchyard and intimidates him into fetching food, brandy, and a blacksmith's file. The boy's simple kindness so impresses the man, coming after the brutality Magwitch has undergone, that he never forgets it. When he amasses a fortune in Australia, he vows to make Pip 'a gentleman'. Magwitch sends mysterious hints to him about money, which Pip fails to understand. He also makes arrangements with Mr Jaggers, his lawyer.

In the meantime Pip has met Miss Havisham of Satis House and her protegee, Estella. Miss Havisham lives in the old house, shut away from the outside world; everything in Satis House remains exactly as it was since the day of Miss Haversham's intended wedding, which was prevented by the bridegroom's failure to appear. Pip finds Estella very attractive, but cold and distant. She has been trained to be so, ready to break men's hearts; but Pip falls in love with her.

When Jaggers, who is also Miss Havisham's lawyer, tells Pip he has "great expectations", Pip assumes that Miss Havisham is his benefactor and that she intends Estella to marry him. Pip's new found wealth turns him into an unfeeling snob. He grows to despise his brother-in-law, the kindly blacksmith, Joe Gargery, who is a natural gentleman. Then, unexpectedly, Magwitch returns. With dismay Pip discovers where his wealth has come from. He also learns that Magwitch, being sentenced to transportation for life, risks death by returning. It then becomes clear that Compeyson, Magwitch's old enemy, is on his trail, eager to denounce Magwitch. Pip discovers, too, that this is the very man who had betrayed Miss Havisham.

Pip's attitudes begin to change. He shrank from Magwitch on the man's return, but gradually Pip comes to respect and even love him, realising that Magwitch has risked his life to come and see him. Then Pip learns that Estella is about to marry the sulky Bentley Drummle; he also discovers that Estella's mother is Jaggers' housekeeper. Jaggers had obtained her acquittal on a murder charge. More startling still, Pip finds that Estella's father is none other than Magwitch.

Pip visits Miss Havisham to ask her to help his friend Pocket. As he leaves the house he suddenly sees flames springing up all around. Pip dashes back to rescue Miss Havisham, whose dress is alight, but she later dies of shock.

Plans are now complete for getting Magwitch onto the Hamburg steamer and away to safety. Pip and Pocket take Magwitch down river. As the packet boat approaches they are suddenly intercepted by a police galley with Compeyson aboard. Magwitch pulls his enemy into the water. The steamer bears down upon them. Compeyson is drowned while Magwitch later dies of his injuries. Pip is seriously ill for a while, and on his recovery goes abroad for eleven years. Returning, he meets Estella in the grounds of Satis House. She is now a widow after an unhappy life with Drummle, but the future of Estella and Pip is left unclear.

In that same month he was faced with another crisis in the sales of his weekly magazine. *A Tale of Two Cities* had been succeeded by Wilkie Collins's *Woman in White*, which proved very popular, but when this had run its course, problems arose. Dickens had hoped to obtain a novel by George Eliot and, when he failed to do so, he was obliged to accept *A Day's Ride: A Life's Romance* by Charles Lever. This turned out to be very dull and not at all to the liking of the readers. This was clearly revealed in the sales figures. Meanwhile Dickens had been quietly mulling over "a very fine, new, and grotesque idea" which had come into his mind and in which he saw all sorts of possibilities. It could be developed, he thought, into one of his involved twenty-part novels. The situation with *All the Year Round* took precedence, however. He wrote to Forster:

It was perfectly clear that the one thing to be done was for me to strike in. I have therefore decided to begin a story, the length of "A Tale of Two Cities", on the First of December ... The name is GREAT EXPECTATIONS. I think a good name?

MRS JOE GARGERY WITH "TICKLER". "*My sister, Mrs Joe Gargery, was more than twenty years older than I* ... '*Mrs Joe*,' *said the blacksmith, 'has been out a dozen times looking for you, Pip, and what's worse, she's got Tickler with her.' Tickler was a wax-ended piece of cane, worn smooth by collision with my tickled frame.*"

Serialisation of this new novel began even before Lever's had been completed. *Great Expectations* took pride of place on the front page while *A Day's Ride* was relegated to the inside. Dickens had to break the news to Lever as tactfully as possible, but he could not hide the facts:

Whether it is too detached and discursive ... I cannot say positively; but it does not take hold ... If the publication were to go steadily down, too long, it would be very very difficult to raise again ... Now do, pray, I entreat you, lay it well to heart that this might have happened with any writer.

The new novel did everything expected of it. Sales of *All the Year Round* rocketed. About 100,000 copies were sold each week. When it was completed, Chapman and Hall issued a library edition in three volumes. It was also published in the United States and Germany. It soon proved to be one of the most popular of Dickens's works, and has retained its popularity ever since.

Yet *Great Expectations* has been called "the grimmest of Dickens's books". It opens on Christmas Eve but there is no hint of a jolly Dickensian Christmas. Instead, it is "on a memorable raw afternoon towards evening" when Pip, the child hero, finds

that this bleak place overgrown with nettles was the churchyard ... and that the dark flat wilderness beyond the churchyard, intersected with dykes and mounds and gates, with scattered cattle feeding on it, was the marshes; and that the low leaden line beyond

ST BARTHOLOMEW THE GREAT. *An ancient church, by Smithfield and Little Britain, well-known to Dickens.*

LONDON DOCKS. *"Down by the docks, you may revolve in a whirlpool of red shirts, shaggy beards, bare tattooed arms, mud, and madness."*

was the river; and that the distant savage lair from which the wind was rushing, was the sea; and that the small bundle of shivers growing afraid of it all and beginning to cry, was Pip.

If this scene were not cold and frightening enough, it is followed at once by the sudden appearance of the convict, Magwitch, "a fearful man, all in coarse grey, with a great iron on his leg", who compels Pip to fetch him a file and "wittles" and threatens that if

he fails or says a word about seeing a man in the graveyard "your heart and your liver shall be tore out, roasted and ate". The next morning Pip manages to bring the food, brandy and file, and watches while Magwitch, shivering from head to foot after spending the night in the open, gobbles down "mincemeat, meat bone, bread, cheese, and pork pie, all at once". Then the boy makes bold to say: "I am glad you enjoy it." This simple observation, this touch of warm human consideration for a criminal who has experienced nothing but ill-treatment, is the hinge on which the story turns. Although he is recaptured, taken back to the hulks and transported to Australia, the convict never forgets it. Later Magwitch tells Pip:

"I see you then a many times as plain as ever I see you on them misty marshes, and I says: Lord, strike me dead, but wot, if I gets liberty and money, I'll make that boy a gentleman!"

And so he does, sending money to Pip secretly through Mr Jaggers, the lawyer. In ignorance of the source of his wealth, Pip employs it to make himself "a gentleman" and is corrupted by it, becoming a snob who

PIP AND THE CONVICT. *" 'You bring me, tomorrow morning early, that file and them wittles. You bring the lot to me at that old battery over yonder . . . You fail, or you go from my words in any partickler, no matter how small it is, and your heart and your liver shall be tore out, roasted, and ate.' " A scene from Cineguild's* Great Expectations, *produced by The Rank Organisation in 1946, and directed by David Lean. Finlay Currie, as Magwitch, and Anthony Wager, as Young Pip, starred in the leading roles.*

is ashamed of the humble folk whom he had known as a child.

I promised myself that I would do something for them one of these days, and formed a plan in outline for bestowing a dinner of roast-beef and plum-pudding, a pint of ale, and a gallon of condescension, upon everybody in the village.

Remaining firmly convinced that the money comes from the eccentric recluse, Miss Havisham, and that she is grooming him to marry Estella, Pip suffers a grievous shock when he discovers the truth. All his pretensions are blown away and, gradually, as he comes to realise the depth of the convict's love for him, and how Magwitch has risked his life by returning to England to see his "gentleman", his views on many things begin to change. In an endeavour to get Magwitch safely away to the Continent after he has been betrayed to the police, Pip and his friend Herbert Pocket make elabo-rate plans to take him by boat down the Thames and get him aboard one of the steamers going to Hamburg or Rotterdam. The attempt fails, Magwitch is injured as the police-galley overhauls the rowing-boat, and he dies in the prison hospital. Pip finds his fortune gone but his vision of the world and his estimate of other people entirely changed.

Of course, *Great Expectations* is much more than this bald outline conveys. It is about money and the true value of money. It is also about class and what is a true gentleman. When he was writing the first instalment, Dickens had told Forster:

I have put a child and a good-natured foolish man, in relations that seem to me very funny.

Joe Gargery, the blacksmith, is the good-natured foolish man but he is also the true gentleman. The book may be, but this is not at all certain, about Ellen Ternan. Estella's name certainly contains part of Ellen's but whether the cold distorted nature of Estella bore any relation to that of Ellen, is doubt-ful. It has been said that "in Estella, we have Dickens's first effective presentation of a sexually attractive girl" (Hobsbaum). Un-doubtedly, there is greater realism in Dick-ens's later heroines but it does not follow that Estella offers any clue to Dickens's relations with Ellen. If *Great Expectations* is

THE YOUNG PIP STRIVES TO PLEASE ESTELLA *while Miss Havisham looks on, in a scene from the 1975 film version produced by Transcontinental. Simon Gipps-Kent played the young Pip, with Sarah Miles as Estella, and Margaret Leighton as Miss Havisham.*

DURING CHRISTMAS DINNER *(below), Pip, having robbed the pantry, anxiously awaits discovery. Another scene from Cineguild's 1946 film,* Great Expectations, *produced by The Rank Organisation.*

MR PUMBLECHOOK, "*A large hard-breathing, middle-aged, slow man, with a mouth like a fish . . .*" *played by Robert Morley (right) in the 1975 Transcontinental production. The cast included James Mason, Anthony Quayle and Joss Ackland.*

WITH ESTELLA AFTER ALL, "*The evening mists were rising now . . . and I saw no shadow of another parting.*"

BY THE LIME-KILNS (*right*). *Pip is lured by the villainous Orlick to the sluice-house on the marshes.*

not necessarily about Ellen Ternan, it is certainly about repentance, which is what so many of his books are about.

Great Expectations was the second of his novels to be written entirely in the first person. (The "Esther's Narrative" chapters of *Bleak House* had also been in the first person.) Unlike *David Copperfield*, however, it was not an autobiography, and only a few of the incidents or descriptions have any bearing on Dickens's own life. Both novels are related by their heroes as they look back upon their experiences, yet there is a distinct difference in each narrator's point of view. David Copperfield is desperately sorry for the boy he had once been:

When my thoughts go back now . . . I seem to see and pity, going on before me, an innocent, romantic boy.

David never repents of having despised his workmates at Murdstone and Grinby's:

Though perfectly familiar with them, my conduct and manner were different enough from theirs to place a space between us. They and the men generally spoke of me as "the little gent".

In contrast, Pip comes to realise how cruelly condescending he has been, and with genuine contrition comes to say:

"Joe and Biddy both . . . receive my humble thanks for all you have done for me, and all I have so ill repaid."

Convicts play an important part in the story of *Great Expectations*. As a boy, Dickens must have been familiar with the sight of them because a great many were employed on the extension to Chatham Dockyard, hence one small item of autobiographical recollection in the novel:

At that time it was customary to carry convicts to the dockyards by stage-coach. As I had . . . more than once seen them on the high road dangling their ironed legs over the coach-roof, I had no cause to be surprised . . . The great numbers on their backs, as if they were street doors; their coarse mangy ungainly outer surface, as if they were lower animals; their ironed legs . . . and the way in which all present looked at them and kept from them; made them . . . a most disagreeable and degraded spectacle.

Many convicts working in the dockyard were housed on hulks in the Medway. There were also hulks in the Thames. Some of them were used as accommodation for prisoners awaiting trial; others for convicts sentenced to transportation. This form of punishment had been seen as a means of unloading the criminal and idle classes upon undeveloped territory where they could start a new and, hopefully, useful life. Originally, convicts had been sent to the

American colonies but when these colonies gained independence this was no longer possible, so they were sent instead to New South Wales, and later to Tasmania (known until 1853 as Van Diemen's Land). Most convicts after a period of good behaviour became ticket-of-leave men and were free to take up employment in the colony. Many remained as settlers, while others, having served their sentence, preferred to return to England. Some, like Magwitch, having been sentenced to transportation for life, were not permitted to return home; if they did so and were caught they were liable to be hanged.

Transportation was not popular with colonists, such as the Micawbers, who had made their homes in these new lands. The convicts in some places often outnumbered the settlers, and their behaviour could be violent and threatening. Those who were convicted of additional crimes might be sent to Norfolk Island to serve their sentence under an especially harsh regime. Such punishment was of little comfort to the genuine settlers who made continual complaints to Westminster about the whole system. With the discovery of gold in Australia, it was generally agreed that the case for keeping criminal trouble-makers as far away from the colonies as possible was overwhelming. Therefore, in 1857, transportation was abolished.

In describing Pip's endeavours to get Magwitch out of the country, Dickens gave some excellent accounts of the Thames just at the time when steam was beginning to supersede sail:

At that time, the steam-traffic on the Thames was far below its present extent, and watermen's boats were far more numerous. Of barges, sailing colliers, and coasting traders, there were perhaps as many as now; but of steamships, great and small, not a tithe or a twentieth part so many.

As Pip and Herbert

went ahead among many skiffs and wherries, briskly, Old London Bridge was soon passed, and old Billingsgate Market with its oyster-boats and Dutchmen, and the White Tower and Traitor's Gate, and [they] were in among the tiers of shipping. Here, were the Leith, Aberdeen, and Glasgow steamers, loading and unloading goods . . . here, were colliers by the score and score, with the coal-whippers plunging off stages on deck, as counterweights to measures of coal swinging up, which were then rattled over the side into barges.

It has been observed how each of these later novels seems to contain a hint given in its predecessor. So, not surprisingly in view of the attention given to the Thames at the close of *Great Expectations*, Dickens's next novel opened with a scene on the river where floated a "dirty and disreputable" boat with two figures in it. However, there was a lengthy period of more than two years before Dickens began this next novel, *Our Mutual Friend*. In that interval he spent much time giving public readings and travelling to most of the larger towns in Great Britain. In January 1863 he even gave three readings at the British Embassy

AT THE ASSEMBLY HALL *where Estella outshone all other beauties, but "this blundering Drummle hung about her." Michael York played the older Pip dancing here with Estella, played by Sarah Miles in the 1975 production.*

OUR MUTUAL FRIEND

John Harmon is heir to a fortune left by his father, a London dust contractor, on condition that he marry Bella Wilfer, a humble clerk's daughter whom John has never seen. On his father's death, John returns from South Africa where he had gone after quarrelling with his father. He is waylaid on the dockside, drugged, and robbed of his belongings by an attacker who is subsequently murdered and his body thrown into the Thames. When John recovers, he realises people believe him to be dead, so he adopts a new name – John Rokesmith – and sets out to assess the character of the girl whom his father had chosen for him. He takes lodgings at the Wilfers's house, where he finds Bella to be a spoilt and self-seeking girl.

With the heir presumed dead, the Harmon property passes to the illiterate Noddy Boffin, who hires the cunning Silas Wegg to read to him every evening. Wegg thus becomes aware of the Harmon affairs and plots to enrich himself. Boffin next engages Rokesmith as his secretary, and invites Bella to come and live in his house, which Bella is pleased to do. Rokesmith sees that Bella is fundamentally a good person and proposes to her, but she rejects him; she wants to marry someone wealthy.

Boffin decides he will reform Bella by pretending to be a miser and disgusting her with his apparent overriding concern for money. Boffin and his wife have in fact recognised their secretary, who has retained many of the mannerisms he had as a small boy. In pursuance of his plan, Boffin accuses John of neglecting his duties and dismisses him. Bella is so incensed at this injustice that she too quits the house and finally accepts John's proposal. John and Bella are married: only later does she learn her husband's true identity.

Meanwhile Wegg has attempted to blackmail Boffin by the purported discovery of papers which would nullify Boffin's possession of most of his property. He is finally thwarted and the tables are turned on him.

A subplot concerns Lizzie Hexham, a waterman's daughter, who attracts the attentions of Eugene Wrayburn, an idle young society man. The unbalanced schoolmaster, Bradley Headstone, is passionately in love with her, and Eugene becomes violently jealous. The climax comes when Headstone attacks Eugene and throws him into the river from which he is rescued, badly injured, by Lizzie. Headstone, meanwhile, has encountered Rogue Riderhood, who has been blackmailing him. During a struggle, both men are drowned in one of the Thames locks. Lizzie nurses Eugene back to health, and they are married despite sneers that she is far from being his social equal.

in Paris. Later he would travel even further.

His success as a reader was phenomenal but he worked extremely hard to achieve it.

I have got the Copperfield reading ready for delivery [he wrote to Wilkie Collins in August 1861] and am now going to blaze away at Nickleby, which I don't like half as well. Every morning I "go in" at these marks for two or three hours, and then collapse and do nothing whatever (counting as nothing much cricket and rounders).

He abridged and amended the original extracts from his novels to make them suitable, and gradually enlarged his repertoire. He found that some of his most popular readings were episodes taken from the special Christmas numbers of *All the Year Round*. Whereas he had begun his reading career in Birmingham with *A Christmas Carol* and *The Cricket on the Hearth*, he now went on to offer a variety of programmes. He not only added the Copperfield and Dotheboys Hall scenes but devised *Mrs Gamp*, *The Trial from Pickwick*, *Dr Marigold*, *Mr Chops the Dwarf* and *The Boy at Mugby*. Towards the close of his life he presented the horrific *Sikes and Nancy*. Each of these readings had to be compiled and rehearsed again and again before they were delivered in public.

Eventually they were all heard by many thousands of people on both sides of the Atlantic. Fortunately, many in his audiences recorded their impressions. There were inevitably a few carping critics who found that Dickens's interpretations of certain characters did not coincide with their own. But the majority were amazed at his versatility and power. One of his great admirers, who attended many of the readings, was the American journalist, Kate Field. In her little book, *Pen Photographs of Dickens's Readings*, she gave detailed descriptions of some of Dickens's techniques. Writing about his readings from *A Christmas Carol*, she noted:

His complete rendering of that dance where "all were top couples at last, and not a bottom one to help them", is owing to the inimitable actions of his hands. They actually perform upon the table, as if it were the floor of Fezziwig's room, and every finger were a leg belonging to one of the Fezziwig family.

Towards the end of his life, Dickens invited an audience of professional actors and actresses who wished to learn how he produced his effects, to come and study him.

They came and he read to them, but they were so transported by the emotions that he evoked that they utterly failed to discover any of his secrets.

These triumphant readings and the continual travelling that they entailed took an immense toll of Dickens's health. He would have been wise to have devoted himself entirely to writing but he was drawn to public reading much as Charles Darnay was drawn to the *Lodestone Rock* of France. Not only was it a money-spinner; it provided excitement, adulation and the intoxicating feeling of having "power". In November 1867 Dickens set out on his second trip to America. He travelled up and down between New York and Washington in dreadful weather giving a series of punishing readings. A few months after his return, he began another reading tour in England and, despite the warnings of his family and friends he introduced the murder scene from *Oliver Twist*. This was an immense strain upon him. Not surprisingly, he broke down in the middle of this tour and had to return home. Yet even after this he could not retire from the platform. He gave a final series of twelve readings in London in the early months of 1870. His last appearance, at St James's Hall, was on Tuesday, 15

DICKENS COMING OUT OF THE PARIS MORGUE *(left)*. *"Whenever I am in Paris, I am dragged by invisible force into the Morgue. One Christmas Day . . . I was attracted in to see an old grey man lying all alone on his cold bed, with a tap of water turned on over his grey hair . . . until it got to the corner of his mouth . . . and made him look sly."*

DICKENS AT HIS DESK. *"Whatever I have tried to do in life, I have tried with all my heart to do well: whatever I have devoted myself to, I have devoted myself completely; in great aims and in small, I have always been thoroughly in earnest."*

THE BONE-GRUBBER *sold bones to the dust contractors who "grew rich on coal-dust, bone-dust, crockery dust — all manner of dust."*

GAFFER HEXAM AND HIS DAUGHTER LIZZIE *are 'in luck'. Gaffer has found another corpse in the Thames.*

OUR MUTUAL FRIEND. *This, Dickens's last completed novel, appeared in twenty monthly parts, illustrated by Marcus Stone. The cover points to several episodes – Gaffer Hexam and Lizzie on the Thames, the dust-contractor, Lizzie dreaming by the fire and other incidents.*

March 1870, and was made memorable by his farewell words to a hushed audience:

From these garish lights I vanish now . . . with a heartfelt, grateful, respectful, affectionate farewell.

That, however, was not to be until several years after the writing and publication of his last twenty-part novel, *Our Mutual Friend*, which came out between April 1864 and November 1865. By this time Dickens was a much slower writer than he had been when he produced *The Pickwick Papers* and *Oliver Twist*. His later manuscripts are a mass of amendments and interlineations. He was also much more aware of the strain of having to deliver a completed amount of text every month by a given date. So he resolved that, with *Our Mutual Friend*, he would have several numbers in hand before the first was published. This seemed to be a successful ploy. He was able to begin the seventh number shortly after the second had appeared on the bookstalls. Very soon, though, he found himself losing ground. To some extent this was due to his poor health at this time. He also had the responsibility of *All the Year Round* and the need to think about the next Christmas number. Added to this was, possibly, his anxiety about the sales of the new work. *Our Mutual Friend* had been advertised in advance on an unprecedented scale. Posters had been displayed in all the London omnibuses, in all the main railway stations and even on Thames steam-launches. Despite this, sales declined number by number, falling from 35,000 to 19,000. Neither public nor critics were very enthusiastic.

Yet, as is now coming to be realised, *Our Mutual Friend* is a very great book indeed. Like many, indeed most, of Dickens's books, it is about money and also about a will. Old John Harmon, a dust contractor, has died before the story opens and has bequeathed his considerable wealth to his son, young John, on condition that he marries Bella Wilfer, the daughter of a poor clerk and a girl whom he has never met. On landing in England from South Africa to take up his inheritance, young John is drugged by the third mate of the ship from which he has just disembarked and his belongings stolen. The mate himself is later attacked and his dead body thrown into the Thames. When it is found and the clothing examined, it is assumed to be young John Harmon's. When John recovers and finds that he is believed to have been murdered, he uses this belief to assume a new identity. As John Rokesmith he sets out to discover the character of the girl whom he has been enjoined to marry. Bella's response on learning that her intended bridegroom is dead is one of dismay at not being able to marry the heir to a fortune.

"There never was such a hard case!" [she declares, almost in tears]. "It was ridiculous enough to have a stranger coming over to marry me whether he liked it or not . . . It was ridiculous enough to know I shouldn't like him . . . left to him in a will, like a dozen spoons . . . These ridiculous points would have been smoothed away by the money, for I love money, and want money – want it dreadfully."

From this beginning the novel traces the stages by which Bella comes to recognise that money is not everything, and the stages of her getting to know "Pa's lodger" – that is, John Rokesmith, alias Harmon – eventually falling in love with him, poor as he apparently is, and consenting to marry him.

This is the thread on which a complex and involved story is hung. The novel introduces a host of characters moving in many contrasting settings. The Harmon fortune has been made out of dust-contracting, in other words, collecting and disposing of refuse from all over London. This could be very lucrative. Not only were the contractors paid to remove refuse from houses and business premises; but after it had been sifted, they had a variety of marketable items – pieces of metal and wood, soot and dung for manure, and many unwanted things which had been thrown away but could be cleaned up and sold. In Dickens's day there were large dust-mounds north of Battle Bridge (where King's Cross station stands today) and at the northern end of Gray's Inn Road. Dickens saw the symbolic use which could be made of these mounds, the equation of dirt and money, to underline the theme of his novel.

The river and riverside characters feature constantly in *Our Mutual Friend*. The story begins with the recovery of a body from the water, the sort of macabre incident which always fascinated Dickens. There are drownings in his books from *Sketches by Boz* onwards. Quilp is drowned. Steerforth is drowned. In an essay from *The Uncommercial Traveller* there is a detailed description of the body of a young woman being taken from the Regent's Canal. In two other essays he recorded what he had seen on visits to the Paris morgue, a place he never failed to visit when he was in the French capital. "Found Drowned" notices also fascinated him. They feature in several novels – in *David Copperfield* and *Bleak House*, for example. One of the funniest scenes in *The Old Curiosity Shop* is where a "Missing – Believed Drowned" notice is being compiled in respect of Quilp, who eavesdrops on arguments concerning the precise description of his various features. These notices have an important role in *Our Mutual Friend*. In an early chapter, Eugene Wrayburn and Mortimer Lightwood visit

the old riverside mill inhabited by Gaffer Hexham, the boatman, and his daughter Lizzie. There they are shown a series of "Found Drowned" notices pasted around the walls. On Lightwood observing that in almost every case the trouser pockets were empty and turned inside out, Hexham nods and confirms:

"But that's common. Now here, *his* pockets was found empty and turned inside out. And here, *her* pocket was found empty and turned inside out."

Many of the riverside scenes are located in the Seven Jolly Fellowship Porters public house, frequented by Rogue Riderhood. The incident where Riderhood is carried

THE DOLLS' DRESSMAKER. " 'I can't get up,' said the child, 'because my back's bad, and my legs are queer.' The dexterity of her nimble fingers was remarkable, and she would glance . . . out of the corners of her grey eyes with a look that out-sharpened all her other sharpness."

THE HAPPY PAIR, *by Marcus Stone. This illustration from* Our Mutual Friend *shows the newly married Lammles, who have just discovered that they were both under the mistaken impression that the other possessed a fortune.* "Do you pretend to believe," *said Mrs Lammle,* "when you talk of my marrying you for worldly advantages, that it was within the bounds of reasonable probability that I would have married you for yourself?"

WESTMINSTER BRIDGE.
*Referred to many times by
Dickens. River steamers set out
from here. Coaches crossed the
bridge en route to Rochester and
Dover.*

unconscious into the public house after a
steamer has run down his wherry in mid-
river is an important one. Dickens seems to
have been unable to get the "Restored to
Life" theme out of his mind. It recurs at
least three times in this novel – once in the
case of John Harmon, then in this incident
with Rogue Riderhood, and later when
Eugene Wrayburn is rescued by Lizzie. In
each case the characters are spared from
drowning but there is a significant difference in the way each man faces the life to

PLEASANT RIDERHOOD "*had it
in the blood to regard seamen,
within certain limits, as her
prey.*"

which he has been restored. Riderhood,
being superstitious, believes that a man restored from drowning cannot be drowned
again. His survival makes no difference to
his life: he remains the same unrepentant
character, which leads to his untimely death
– by drowning – at the end of the book.
Wrayburn, by contrast, acknowledges the
mistakes of his past life. He treats his im-
mersion in the river as a type of baptism, a
sign of being born again. He lives to marry
Lizzie Hexham. Thus, like so many of Dickens's later novels, this one is basically about
repentance.

Great Ormond Street Children's Hospital
provided another setting. It is the scene of
the death of little Johnny. Dickens took a
great interest in this hospital and gave
several readings in aid of its funds. His
description of a visit to the little boy's bed-
side is one of the most touching things that
he ever wrote, and is much more natural
than the death of Paul Dombey. Johnny's
visitors found that he

had become one of a little family, all in little quiet
beds (except two playing dominoes in little arm-chairs
at a little table on the hearth); and on all the little beds
were little platforms whereon were to be seen dolls'
houses, woolly dogs with mechanical barks ... tin
armies, Moorish tumblers, wooden tea-things, and
the riches of the earth.

Dickens renewed his attack on the Poor
Law through little Johnny's grandmother,
eighty-year-old Betty Higden, "who by dint
of an indomitable purpose and a strong
constitution" has been able to fight against
the Poor Law and retain her independence
for many years, even "though each year has
come with its new knock-down blows fresh
to the fight against her". Her great dread is
to end her life in an almshouse:

"Do I never read in the newspapers," she asks, "...
how the worn-out people get driven from post to
pillar and pillar to post? Do I never read ... how they
are grudged, grudged, grudged the shelter, or the
doctor, or the drop of physic, or the bit of bread?"

Our Mutual Friend also has something to
say about another of Dickens's concerns –
Ragged Schools. In the chapter entitled "Of
an Educational Character" there is a lurid
description of one. It was held in

a miserable loft in an unsavoury yard. Its atmosphere
was oppressive and disagreeable; it was crowded,

noisy, and confusing . . . Its teachers, animated solely by good intentions, had no idea of execution, and a lamentable jumble was the upshot of their kind endeavours . . . All the place was pervaded by a pretence that every pupil was childish . . . Young women old in the vices of the commonest and worst life were expected to profess themselves enthralled by the Adventures of Little Margery . . .'

Our Mutual Friend contains many amusing passages. The most brilliant is surely the scene at the dinner-party when Mr Podsnap encounters the foreign gentleman. Mr Podsnap, we are informed,

considered other countries a mistake, and of their manners and customs would conclusively observe, "Not English!" when PRESTO! with a flourish of the arm, and a flush of the face, they were swept away.

Therefore, on being introduced to the foreign gentleman, Mr Podsnap addresses him as if he were administering a potion to a deaf child, and enquires whether the gentleman has found London to be "Very Rich". The foreign gentleman finds it, without doubt, "énormément riche".

"Enormously Rich, We say," returns Mr Podsnap, in a condescending manner. "Our English adverbs do NOT terminate in Mong, and we pronounce the "ch" as if there were a "t" before it. We say Ritch."

Our Mutual Friend itself is too enormously rich for anyone to do it justice in a few hundred words. It would have been a great tragedy if this book had come to a prema-

ture end. But that is what nearly happened. On Friday, 9 June 1865, Dickens was involved in a "terribly destructive" railway accident at Staplehurst. His carriage was the only one which did not topple off the viaduct into the field below. He managed to get out unhurt and do what he could to

THE EVIL GENIUS OF THE HOUSE OF BOFFIN. *Mr Wegg plots to ruin Mr Boffin. "There'll shortly be an end of you."*

CHANGING HOUSE, by George Edgar Hicks. This picture shows the wedding party of a "new" family such as the Veneerings in Our Mutual Friend. *Dickens's satire was directed at the* nouveaux riches *who were invading society in the 1860s. "Mr and Mrs Veneering were bran-new people in a bran-new house in a bran-new quarter of London. Everything about the Veneerings was spick and span new."*

THE MYSTERY OF EDWIN DROOD

Edwin Drood is a young man whose father's dying wish was that Edwin should marry Rosa Bud, the daughter of his closest friend and a pupil of Miss Twinkleton at Cloisterham. Neither Rosa nor Edwin is pleased about the arranged engagement, but they do not formally renounce it. Edwin's uncle, John Jasper, the opium-addicted choirmaster of Cloisterham Cathedral, is secretly in love with Rosa. Neville Landless from Ceylon is also attracted to her. He and his twin sister are dark, lithe and mysterious; the sister is known to have dressed in male attire on one occasion. Neville strongly resents Edwin's casual treatment of Rosa, and they quarrel. Lawyer Grewgious is also concerned about Edwin's attitude to the girl. He gives Edwin a ring to be handed to Rosa if and when they become solemnly committed to each other; otherwise, Edwin is to return the ring to Grewgious.

On Christmas Eve, Neville and Edwin meet with Jasper in his house, ostensibly to try and reconcile their antagonism. Neville starts out on a walking tour the next day, but when Drood cannot be found, he is pursued and brought back. Later he is released for lack of evidence. Then Edwin's watch and shirt-pin are discovered by the river. A stranger, Datchery, arrives in Cloisterham. He is apparently someone in disguise, whose purpose is to watch Jasper's movements. But his true identity, and answers to the puzzles whether Drood had merely disappeared or had actually been murdered, remain undisclosed, since Dickens died leaving the novel unfinished.

help the injured. Then he climbed back into the carriage to rescue his manuscript which was "much soiled, but otherwise unhurt". In the postscript that he added to the completed novel, he wrote:

I remember with devout thankfulness that I can never be much nearer parting company with my readers for ever than I was then.

The shock to his system resulting from this accident was very serious, however, and in some respects he never fully recovered from it. His health began to deteriorate and was not improved by the arduous reading tour of the United States in 1867 and 1868. In July 1869 he began to mull over notions for another book.

What should you think [he asked Forster] of the idea of a story beginning in this way? Two people, boy and girl, or very young, going apart from one another, pledged to be married after many years – at the end of the book.

It was another start from the previous book: a variation on John Harmon's will and the planned marriage of young John to Bella Wilfer. A month later, however, Dickens again wrote to Forster:

I laid aside the fancy I told you of, and have a very curious and new idea for my new story. Not a communicable idea (or the interest of the book would be gone), but a very strong one, though difficult to work.

It is a pity that Dickens did not find his ideas for *The Mystery of Edwin Drood* communicable, because he died before the book was completed and, despite many attempts to do so, the *Mystery* remains a mystery to this day. Dickens offered to divulge it to Queen Victoria when he was honoured with an audience on 9 March 1870 but she showed no curiosity and their talk was taken up discussing servant problems and photographs of the American Civil War that Dickens had brought to show her. John Forster obtained some information, fortunately, and left it on record that the story

was to be that of a murder of a nephew by his uncle; the originality of which was to consist in the review of the murderer's career by himself at the close, when its temptations were to be dwelt upon as if, not he the culprit, but some other man, were the tempted. The last chapter was to be written in the condemned cell.

Dickens began to write *The Mystery of Edwin Drood* in October 1869 and the first number appeared in April 1870. It was not conceived as another of his lengthy novels. It was to be concluded in twelve parts and would be illustrated by Luke Fildes. When Dickens died on 9 June 1870, only sufficient for six parts had been completed.

Much ingenuity has been employed to

JASPER'S GATEHOUSE. "*There is little stir or movement after dark. There is little enough in the high tide of the day, but there is next to none at night . . . One might fancy that the tide of life was stemmed by Mr Jasper's own Gatehouse. The murmur of the tide is heard beyond; but no wave passes the archway, over which his lamp burns red behind the curtain, as if the building were a Lighthouse.*"

A LASCARS' DEN, by Gustave Doré. "*The meanest and closest of small rooms . . . He lies, dressed, across a large unseemly bed . . . Lying, also dressed and also across the bed, not longwise, are a Chinaman, a Lascar, and a haggard woman. The two first are in a sleep or stupor; the last is blowing at a kind of pipe, to kindle it.*"

APPLICANTS AWAITING ADMISSION TO THE CASUAL WARD, BY LUKE FILDES (1844–1927). " 'Why, Lord bless my soul, what am I to do? What can I do? The place is full. The place is always full – every night. I must give preference to women with children, mustn't I? You wouldn't have me not do that?' "

A DANGEROUS MOMENT (*right*). *"Edwin Drood's face has been quickly and remarkably flushed by the wine; so has the face of Neville Landless." A scene from the startlingly atmospheric film production by Universal in 1934. Claude Rains, Heather Angel and Douglas Montgomery starred in the leading roles.*

IN THE OPIUM DEN (*far right*). *'Ye've smoked as many as five since ye came in at midnight. O me, O me, my lungs is weak!'*

unravel the various mysteries that are presented in this unfinished fragment. The first one is whether Drood was really murdered – or did he just disappear? A number of writers have challenged Forster's categorical statement that Drood was killed. They point out that the book's title is *The Mystery* not *The Murder of Edwin Drood*. In fact, we know that Dickens pointed this out to one of his own family and, as he had a propensity to keep repeating the "restored to life" theme in one novel after another, it is not at all unreasonable to suppose that Drood was intended to return in some mysterious way. The bottom picture of the cover to each monthly part shows a man

with a lantern throwing its beam upon the figure of another man discovered in some dark cellar, or possibly a grotto or crypt. Might this not be Edwin Drood, alive when everyone believes him dead? The drawings in the cover were the work of Dickens's son-in-law, Charles Collins, who received careful instructions about what each part of

the cover-design should contain; unfortunately, however, Dickens did not explain to him precisely what the pictures signified.

Against this conjecture is the evidence of Luke Fildes, who asked Dickens why it was important that Jasper should be portrayed wearing a double neck-tie. Dickens is said to have replied:

Can you keep a secret? I must have the double neck-tie. It is necessary because Jasper strangles Edwin Drood with it.

Various experts have pointed out that the Thugs, the followers of Kali, strangled their victims in this way, and there are indications throughout the novel of thuggee. Against all these arguments, however, is the possibility that Drood was indeed strangled, but not killed. In *Barnaby Rudge* the steward Rudge was believed to have been murdered yet proved to be alive. In *Our Mutual Friend* John Harmon was believed to have been murdered but turned up alive. Could not the same basic plot be repeated in *The Mystery of Edwin Drood*?

The cover-page, drawn by Collins, has been the subject of very close scrutiny and argument, though much of it is perfectly plain. There is no mistaking Jasper and Rosa Bud in the garden, nor Edwin and Rosa in the cathedral. The bottom corner pictures are obviously the opium den visited by Jasper in the opening chapter. In reality this was a den that Dickens had visited in Shadwell, where he took note of the things that he was to describe in the novel – the opium-pipes made from penny ink-bottles and the ejaculated phrases from the half-drugged woman who filled the pipes and puffed at them until the opium was aglow.

Much of the action in *The Mystery of Edwin Drood* takes place in the cathedral city of Cloisterham. This is a thin disguise for Rochester, where any visitor can quickly identify many of the buildings which Dickens describes. To start with there is the lodging of John Jasper:

an old stone gatehouse crossing the Close, with an arched thoroughfare passing underneath it. Through its latticed window, a fire shines out upon the fast darkening scene.

Then there is Minor Canon Row, which Dickens renamed Minor Canon Corner:

a quiet place in the shadow of the Cathedral, which the cawing of the rooks, the echoing steps of rare passers, the sound of the Cathedral bell, or the roll of the Cathedral organ, seemed to render more quiet than absolute silence.

Eastgate House Dickens renamed the Nuns' House, and it is now the Dickens Centre:

In the midst of Cloisterham stands the Nuns' House; a venerable brick edifice, whose present appellation is doubtless derived from the legend of its conventual uses. On the trim gate enclosing its old courtyard is a resplendent brass plate flashing forth the legend: "Seminary for Young Ladies, Miss Twinkleton".

Finally there is the great cathedral which dominates the book as it does the city. Here came Mr Grewgious, the lawyer. Crossing the close, he

paused at the great western folding-door of the Cathedral, which stood open on the fine and bright, though short-lived, afternoon, for the airing of the place.

WEST DOOR, ROCHESTER CATHEDRAL *(left and above). In his* Week's Tramp in Dickens Land, *W.R. Hughes recorded that "The Norman west front has a richly sculptured door of five receding arches, containing figures of the Saviour and the twelve apostles, and statues of Henry I and his Queen, Matilda." The figures are now suffering badly from erosion.*

STAPLE INN HALL. *"Staple Inn . . . is one of those nooks which are legal nooks; and it contains a little Hall, with a little lantern in its roof."*

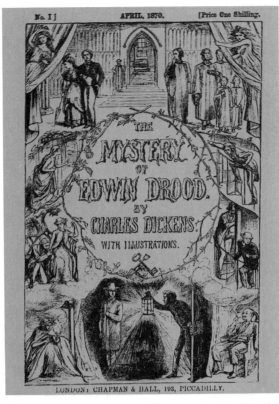

"Dear me," said Mr Grewgious, peeping in, "it's like looking down the throat of Old Time."

Old Time heaved a mouldy sigh from tomb and arch and vault; and gloomy shadows began to deepen in corners, and damps began to rise from green patches of stone; and jewels, cast upon the pavement of the nave from the stained glass by the declining sun, began to perish. Within the grill-gate of the chancel, up the steps surmounted loomingly by the fast darkening organ, white robes could be dimly seen, and one feeble voice, rising and falling in a cracked monotonous mutter, could at intervals be faintly heard. In the free outer air the river, the green pastures, and the brown arable lands, the teeming hills and dales, were reddened by the sunset; while the distant little windows in windmills and farm homesteads, shone, patches of bright beaten gold.

Some critics have suggested that Dickens had lost his touch when he came to write this novel. Even Wilkie Collins called this novel "the melancholy work of a worn-out brain". Such passages as the one just quoted prove such criticisms to be wrong. Dickens was still in command of all his wonderful faculties for invention, description and characterisation, and was even breaking new ground in style and presentation. John Jasper must surely rank as one of his most complex and carefully drawn characters, at once mysterious, difficult to fathom and ambivalent. Luke Honeythunder is another character who deserves attention, although very few critics have bothered to give any. He is an anticipation of all those terrible Communist dictators whose honeyed words have promised Utopia and the brotherhood of man, and whose thunder has constantly threatened the world with war. He is a man intent upon seizing his fellow-creatures "by the scruff of the neck and . . . bumping them into the paths" of philanthropy. His philanthropy, as Dickens explains, was "of that gunpowderous sort that the difference between it and animosity was hard to determine".

Mysteries abound in *Edwin Drood* – modern versions should perhaps be re-titled *The Mysteries of Edwin Drood*. Was Drood murdered and, if so, how and why? If he was not murdered, what became of him? Who was the enigmatic Datchery who suddenly arrived in Cloisterham? Did Jasper practice mesmerism and, if so, what part was it to play in the story? Was there some secret connection between Jasper and the old hag, Princess Puffer, of the opium den? What exactly happened to Durdles on the previous Christmas Eve when he took Jasper on a moonlight expedition among the "tombs, vaults, towers and ruins"? Nor does this by any means exhaust the catalogue of mysteries which still await their solution in this puzzling and fascinating book. Although it was never finished and the mysteries cannot be solved, it is still a novel worth reading.

As Longfellow said: "It is certainly one of his most beautiful works, if not the most beautiful of all."

DICKENS'S ACHIEVEMENTS

CHAPTER
6

DICKENS'S ACHIEVEMENTS

On 8 June 1870, Dickens varied his usual routine. He spent the morning writing in his chalet as he always did when he was at Gad's Hill. At lunchtime he returned to the house for a light meal but then, unexpectedly, he went back to the chalet and for the remainder of the afternoon continued writing *The Mystery of Edwin Drood*. Before dinner he wrote several letters in his library and then joined his sister-in-law, Georgina Hogarth, at the dinner-table. She was alarmed by his appearance and asked whether he was well. He said that he had been very ill for the last hour. He then declared he must go to London at once. He stood up from the table but could hardly keep upright and would have fallen if Georgina had not come quickly to support him. She tried to get him to the sofa but he muttered: "On the floor". These were his last words. He died the next day at ten minutes past six in the evening. A few days later he was buried in Poets' Corner at Westminster Abbey.

Dickens was a phenomenal worker. He wrote thousands of letters, many of them full of humorous anecdotes and graphic descriptions. For twenty years he edited a weekly magazine. He spent many weeks producing and acting in plays, and many more weeks and months travelling about giving public readings. These activities in themselves would have been sufficient to occupy the lives of most ordinary men but for Dickens they were merely extra activities. His life-work was writing.

The previous chapters have given some idea of his output. He left the world fifteen

PORTRAIT OF DICKENS BY WILLIAM POWELL FRITH (*far left*). *Frith delayed working on this portrait in the hope that Dickens would shave off the moustache ("the hideous disfigurement") that he had recently grown. Instead, Dickens added a beard, so the painting went ahead. When Landseer saw it he remarked: "I wish he looked less eager and busy. I should like to catch him asleep and quiet now and then."*

DICKENS'S GRAVE IN WESTMINSTER ABBEY. *Early in the morning of 14 June 1870, Dickens was buried in Poets' Corner. Only members of the family and a few close friends were present. As the brief service was held, the statue of Shakespeare fittingly appeared to look down. Later, as Dean Stanley recorded: "There was a constant pressure to the spot, and many flowers were strewn upon it by unknown hands, many tears shed from unknown eyes."*

SIX OF DICKENS'S
ILLUSTRATORS. *Top (left to
right): Robert Seymour, Sir Luke
Fildes, R.W. Buss; bottom,
George Cruikshank, Marcus
Stone, H.K. Browne (Phiz).*

OLIVER AMAZED *at the craft of
the Artful Dodger (opposite,
bottom left). By characterising
thieves and other criminals in his
novels, Dickens was able to
highlight the problems they
presented.*

major novels, five Christmas books, two travel books, two books of essays and sketches, plus several stories written in collaboration with others, for example *No Thoroughfare* and *The Lazy Tour of Two Idle Apprentices*, written with Wilkie Collins, and fourteen Christmas numbers of his magazines written by various hands including his own. There is also a substantial body of miscellaneous pieces: *A Child's History of England, The Mudfog Papers, Sketches of Young Gentlemen, Sketches of Young Couples,* and *The Life of our Lord.* Then there are little-known books edited by Dickens – *The Life of Grimaldi* and *The Religious Opinions of the Reverend Chauncey Hare Townshend.*

After Shakespeare, Dickens is the greatest name in English literature, although it has taken a little time for this to be generally recognised. Immediately after his death, his reputation declined. He was derided for his sentimentality, his alleged exaggeration and his inability to portray believable women. Critics were so busy pointing out his faults that they failed to see his virtues. In the years before 1939, however, opinions began to change. Essays by George Orwell and Edmund Wilson heralded a new era in the appreciation of Dickens, and since then Dickens (a little grudgingly at times) has been accorded his rightful place.

It is probable that Dickens is much better known to the general public today than Shakespeare is. In Dickens's time, owing to the practice in middle-class households of reading aloud to the family, Shakespeare was as familiar to the reading public as was the Bible, and pictures of his characters would have been identified immediately. Today it is doubtful whether the man in the street would recognise many at all – very few beyond Shylock, Hamlet, Falstaff, Prince Hal, Macbeth and perhaps Puck and Bottom. Irrespective of whether he had read any Dickens novels or not, he would be able to name Mr Pickwick, Sam Weller, Mrs Gamp, Squeers, Pecksniff, Quilp, Captain

Cuttle and many more such characters.

Not only would he recognise their appearance, he would recognise their sayings: that Uriah Heep was 'umble, that Oliver Twist asked for more and that Mr Micawber was always waiting for something to turn up. People who have never opened *A Tale of Two Cities* know that it begins: "It was the best of times, it was the worst of times" and concludes: "It is a far, far better thing I do than I have ever done". With *A Christmas Carol* being broadcast and dramatised so often, everyone is familiar with Scrooge's snarl: "Bah! Humbug!" But even the less well-known of Dickens's books have added quotations to the common stock. Not everyone remembers all of Mrs General's speech (in *Little Dorrit*):

"The word Papa, besides, gives a pretty form to the lips. Papa, potatoes, poultry, prunes, and prism are all very good words for the lips; especially prunes and prism."

But most people have heard of "Prunes and prism".

As a writer Dickens has greatly influenced other writers. His influence is most clearly seen in the work of Shaw, Wells and Priestley, but it extended to Joyce and T.S. Eliot, to Wodehouse, and even to writers of boys' stories such as Frank Richards, creator of Billy Bunter and the Famous Five of

Greyfriars School. He had an equally great influence on foreign writers, and not merely the Americans: Tolstoy, Gogol and Dostoevsky had all read and enjoyed Dickens and absorbed some of his style and techniques.

A constant experimentation is discernible in Dickens's work. He moved forward constantly, despite popular pressure to reproduce books like *The Pickwick Papers*. He greatly extended the range of subjects with which a novelist might deal. While always careful to observe the proprieties of language and description, he was quite prepared to ignore disapproval and introduce thieves and prostitutes into his stories. Their speech may not always be convincing but they are presented as the genuine articles and not as romantic figures. Dickens was thus able to discuss the problems they presented to society in a way acceptable to his rather prim readers.

Dickens was an experimenter in other ways. His use of symbols to deepen his meaning – the fog in *Bleak House*, the sea in *Dombey and Son* and the dust-heaps in *Our Mutual Friend* – is an innovation. He also experimented with grammar. The description of the fog just mentioned is given in a long paragraph without a single verb. Several purists objected to what they regarded as misuse of the language, and not many of those who appreciated the effect

DICKENS'S DREAM, *BY ROBERT W. BUSS, a well-known artist who was engaged to illustrate* The Pickwick Papers *after Seymour's suicide. He had no experience of etching, however, and his inability led to the two plates that he provided being, in his own words "abominably bad". He was curtly dismissed by Chapman and Hall.*

THE HALL CLOCK AT GAD'S HILL PLACE. *Dickens complained to his clockmaker that after being cleaned the clock had failed to strike. "If you can send down any confidential person with whom the clock can confer, I think it may have something on its works that it would be glad to make a clean breast of."*

Dickens had thereby gained were ready to recommend it as the correct way to write English.

Little Dorrit contains another interesting example of Dickens's innovations. The need was to describe a gathering of professional men. To have given each an individual name would have been tedious. To have written "The accountant said this" and "The surgeon said that" would have been clumsy. Dickens solved the problem in his own inimitable way.

Admiralty said Mr Merdle was a wonderful man. Treasury said he was a new power in the country . . . Bishop said he was glad to think that this wealth flowed into the coffers of a gentleman who was always disposed to maintain the best interests of Society.

It is strange that many people fail to realise that Dickens originally made his name as a humorist. There are people who say they find Dickens so sad that they can hardly read him at all. It is certainly true there is a great deal of pathos in his books, and this was relished by his first readers. The deaths of Little Nell and Paul Dombey reduced both England and America to tears. Later, the plight of Jo the crossing-sweeper and little orphan Johnny touched the hearts of thousands. But the humour of Dickens outweighs the pathos, and there are all sorts of humour. There is the slap-stick of Mr Winkle's attempts to mount a horse or skate on a pond. There is the worldly wisdom of Sam Weller with his racy stories and "Wellerisms", such as "There's

nothin' so refreshin' as sleep, sir, as the servant girl said afore she drank the eggcup-ful of laudanum". There is the sly satire as in the gathering of professional gentlemen mentioned above. There are the thousands of similes which are scattered throughout everything he wrote. Even when he responds to a situation with pity or horror, Dickens's sense of humour cannot be wholly suppressed. Little Oliver Twist is given a bed in the undertaker's shop where his eyes light on a row of elm-boards cut into the shape of coffin-lids, "looking in the dim light, like high-shouldered ghosts with their hands in their breeches-pockets". When Dickens visited the Zoo and saw the snakes being fed with live birds, he described one of the reptiles "looking back over half a yard of shoulder".

It was his ability to make readers laugh and cry which made him so popular an author. He could also arouse pity and indignation, which made him so effective a protagonist for reform. As we have seen, he drew attention to the ludicrous practice of imprisonment for debt, to the inhuman conditions in the new workhouses, to the cruelty meted out to forgotten children in Yorkshire schools, to the scandal of government maladministration and to the horrors

of public executions. His campaigns were conducted not only in his fictions but in articles that he either wrote himself or commissioned from others for *Household Words* and *All the Year Round*. Although he did not always succeed in bringing about reforms immediately, he sowed the seed for future improvements by bringing matters to the attention of the public and of politicians.

Dickens's achievements as writer and reformer were therefore very considerable. There is, however, a danger of his real achievement being forgotten. In recent years scholars have been examining his works from every angle, puzzling out the time-scheme of his novels, suggesting where he obtained or borrowed his ideas, commenting on the rhythm of his emotional passages, pontificating on his treatment of minor characters, and so on. Others have been delving into his personal history, seeking the advice of psychiatrists on aspects of his behaviour, scanning his letters and notebooks for clues about his inner being, recording in meticulous details where he was from day to day, and doing everything possible to throw light on his relationship with Ellen Ternan.

This concentration on matters that are

really inessential has resulted in the neglect of the essential. What was Dickens all about? What did he spend his life doing? What is the thread which runs through all his work? The Victorians, of course, had no doubt about it. Dickens was striking mighty blows for the poor. He was preaching the love of humanity. He was asking people to be kind and thoughtful towards one another. He was trying to make Christmas stay with us the whole year round ("*All the Year Round*"?) because, as he said, "when it begins to do so, we shall make this earth a very different place". With all his faults, for all his devious behaviour, these are the things that Dickens was trying to do and which in great measure he succeeded in doing. This was his achievement, and we, in our cynical age, should not overlook it.

BOB CRATCHIT AND TINY TIM. *"And in came little Bob, the father with at least three feet of comforter . . . hanging down before him, and Tiny Tim upon his shoulder. Alas, for Tiny Tim, he bore a little crutch, and had his limbs supported by an iron frame."*

DICKENS IN NEW YORK *(left) photographed by Gurney in 1868, wearing a quilted overcoat and holding his top-hat.*

DICKENSIANA

ROYAL DOULTON TOBY JUGS
(top right), depicting Pickwickian
characters. From left to right:
Sam Weller, modelled by Charles
Noke and Harry Fenton, 1940–
1960; Buzfuz, modelled by
Harry Fenton, 1948–1960; Mr
Pickwick, modelled by Charles
Noke and Harry Fenton,
1940–1960.

A SET OF PUNCH LADELS (centre
right). These ladles, each
surmounted by a character from
The Pickwick Papers, were
presented to Dickens by his
publishers, Chapman and Hall,
at a dinner at the Prince of
Wales, to mark the completion of
the novel which had been
published in twenty monthly
parts.

MONTHLY PARTS COVER OF
DOMBEY AND SON (bottom right).
Illustrated by Phiz, this green
cover depicts the general theme of
the novel. Proud Mr Dombey
with eyes closed is oblivious to the
insecurity of the money, ledgers
and cash-boxes on which he
banks, but which are really akin
to a house of cards.

ROYAL DOULTON FIGURINES
(bottom centre). These unusual
statuettes, modelled by Leslie
Harradine, depict some of the
most memorable Dickensian
characters with all their
mannerisms and idiosyncracies.
From left to right, Mrs Gamp,
Pecksniff, Mr Micawber, Uriah
Heep, Mr Pickwick and Fat Boy.

CERAMIC STATUETTE PORTRAYING DICKENS *in characteristic pose at his reading desk (far left).*

A POSTCARD *illustrating a scene from* Bleak House, c. 1920. *"We have among us my friends . . . a brother and a boy. Devoid of parents, devoid of relations, devoid of flocks and herds, devoid of gold and silver, and of precious stones."*

TOBY JUGS BY ROYAL DOULTON, *depicting Dickensian characters. Dickens provided such detailed descriptions of his characters that many figurines have been based on the more memorable character-types. These Royal Doulton toby jugs are greatly prized by collectors. Each about 3 cm in height, they were issued to celebrate the 170th anniversary of Dickens's birth.*

CIGARETTE CARDS *illustrated by Kyd, c. 1920, popularised the great Dickensian character-types (bottom left).*

143

INDEX